Teaching The Little, Brown Reader

Tenth Edition

Edited by

Marcia Stubbs

Sylvan Barnet

William E. Cain

PEARSON
Longman

New York   Boston   San Francisco
London   Toronto   Sydney   Tokyo   Singapore   Madrid
Mexico City   Munich   Paris   Cape Town   Hong Kong   Montreal

Senior Sponsoring Editor: Virginia L. Blanford
Senior Supplements Editor: Donna Campion
Electronic Page Makeup: Dianne Hall

Instructor's Handbook to accompany *The Little, Brown Reader*, Tenth Edition by Marcia
Stubbs, Sylvan Barnet, and William E. Cain.

ISBN: 0-321-33076-5

1 2 3 4 5 6 7 8 9 10—OPM—08 07 06 05

CONTENTS

8 Teaching and Learning   85

ACKNOWLEDGMENTS

Dr. Johnson famously said that a writer "will turn over half a library to make one book," and it sometimes did seem that we were turning over half a library in our efforts to find good material for *The Little, Brown Reader*. This business of reading didn't surprise us; what did surprise us is that in the course of writing the pages for this supplementary guide, we found we were turning over the other half of the library. But most surprising of all was our discovery that our manuscript, which we thought was in good shape when we submitted it to the publisher, benefited immensely from editorial assistance provided by the publisher.

Here we want to record our thanks for the amazingly helpful editorial assistance that we received: Donna Campion, Senior Supplements Editor at Longman, kept the project moving; Dianne Hall did a remarkable job in handling the complexities of the electronic page makeup; and Chrysta Meadowbrooke, our copyeditor and proofreader, peppered the pages with queries that made us revise, revise again, and revise yet again—that is, she asked us to do exactly what we ask our students to do. We hope that all teachers get such professional help with their publications, and we hope that we, as teachers of composition, offer comparable help to our students.

MARCIA STUBBS
SYLVAN BARNET
WILLIAM E. CAIN

A NOTE ON
USING THE PICTURES

We include twenty-five pictures in *The Little, Brown Reader (LBR)*, two preceding each thematic section and nine in Chapter 5, an essay entitled "Reading and Writing about Pictures." (Chapter 5 itself includes an essay by a student, describing and analyzing a photograph.)

The pictures preceding each section are, we think, handsome to look at, but we have also included them to provide for short writing assignments based on visual (as opposed to printed) texts or the comparison of visual and printed texts. Describing and analyzing visual texts is often an excellent introduction to critical thinking and writing. Students are attracted to pictures and have an immediate response to them, often a more expert response than they have to printed texts. But to write about a picture, the writer must look at the picture again, and then again, questioning his or her responses to it, analyzing the components of the picture to explain (and often to revise) those responses, searching for the details of the picture and the language to describe the details to support the analysis. It is this process, and some of the special language for writing about pictures, that we take up in Chapter 5.

The pictures we include, and others that students themselves find, can be used for a variety of writing assignments. Here are five suggestions.

1. If students are keeping journals, the pictures beginning a section can be proposed or assigned for journal entries. Since the pictures and readings are thematically linked, these entries often provide ideas for essays on the topics suggested by the readings.

2. Students can be encouraged to freewrite on a picture. The freewriting often leads to astute critical perceptions, usually on the picture's content or theme, but sometimes on the formal composition of the picture as well.

3. A highly successful writing exercise requires only two paragraphs; it requires students to describe a picture in one paragraph and to analyze or respond to it in the second paragraph. Here's one way to word the assignment:

   > Choose a picture from *The Little, Brown Reader* to describe and analyze. Your essay will require only two paragraphs, but each paragraph should be substantial. In your first paragraph identify the picture (artist's name, place, and date of publication) and describe the picture well enough so that someone who has not seen it can visualize or even draw a sketch of it fairly accurately. In a second paragraph interpret, analyze, and respond to the picture. What does the artist or photographer seem to be saying by means of the picture? How does he or she convey the picture's theme (the idea or emotion)? To what in the picture do you most deeply respond, or why did you choose this picture to write about?

The exercise teaches several things: description is not the same thing as analysis (just as summary is not the same as analysis); a description must be specific, and as complete and accurate as possible (if you want some-one to see what you have seen); and a description must follow some orga-nizing principle if it is to be easily grasped by someone who is not look-ing at the object but reading your words about it.

An amusing class hour can demonstrate some of these points. With a student's draft of the descriptive paragraph in hand, ask for a volunteer to go to the blackboard. Another student, not the writer of the paragraph, reads the paragraph from beginning to end aloud to the class (omitting the identification of the picture). Then the reader goes back to read it a sentence at a time, so that the student at the board can draw a sketch. Other students can look at the picture in *LBR* but are not allowed to sup-ply hints. The person drawing can be instructed only by the reader, who can only repeat from the paragraph whatever the drawer wants to hear again. It soon becomes evident if important details have been omitted or inaccurately described. The need for such words as "on the left," "behind the first figure," "in the foreground," and so on, becomes equally evident. The class learns something about writing description, about organizing paragraphs, about using transitions. Above all, the lesson is: your readers cannot know what you see (or think) unless you take the pains to tell them. And now, the writer can read his or her draft of the second para-graph, and the class can discuss it, or you can repeat the exercise with a second paragraph of description.

4. Students can be asked to write a brief caption for a picture, consisting of two or three sentences. This is an exercise in description, analysis, and summary. If students write captions for pictures they have described and analyzed in two paragraphs (as in the previous exercise), they now practice presenting concisely (summarizing) their most significant findings. Writing a caption is similar to writing a thesis sentence for a longer essay.

5. Research papers can be based on a photographer represented in the text—Lange, for example, or Cartier-Bresson. Or a paper can be written on the Farm Security Administration which sponsored some of the pho-tographs by Lange and Wolcott.

You will find other suggestions for assignments based on pictures in this manual, in which we discuss each picture in order of its appearance in the text. We don't expect anyone to give more than a few writing assignments based on pictures, but we know that students enjoy these assignments and we believe that they profit from them. Writing about pictures also provides a nice change of pace from writing about printed texts, and since most students are relatively good at it, it helps to boost classroom morale.

If you ask students to write about any of the pictures in *LBR*, you may want to provide them with this checklist as a way to stimulate ideas.

Reading and Writing about Pictures: A Checklist

1. What is the subject matter of the picture? What, if anything, is happening?

2. If there are figures, what (if anything) is the relationship between them? How is it expressed pictorially?

3. If the picture is a photograph, does it seem to be a snapshot, interesting in part because of a messy vitality, or does it seem to be carefully posed, interesting in part because of its formality?

4. To what degree, if any, do you take the picture to be a document of the period? What, if anything, does it tell you about the period?

5. What in the picture evokes the response you have? Why do you find the picture amusing or moving or boring or whatever?

A NOTE ON
USING THE SHORT VIEWS

Each thematic section of *The Little, Brown Reader* contains, following the two pictures, a group of brief statements entitled "Short Views." These range from epigrammatic sentences to a few paragraphs. Often the views are controversial, and sometimes contrasting or opposing views are juxtaposed.

Again, as with the pictures, Short Views can be used in a variety of ways to stimulate writing. Students can comment on them in journal entries, or they can respond, in freewriting, to a Short View, especially to one they disagree with (perhaps without knowing why). Short Views can be compared, or students can compose a Short View to contrast with one they disagree with or disapprove of. A practice we have found useful is to start a class hour by asking students to take turns reading aloud the Short Views from the unit they're working on. When we've done this we have noticed how few students nowadays can read aloud with any comfort, probably because they have seldom been asked to read aloud or had anyone read aloud to them. We think that reading aloud is a good way to learn to pay attention to a text—the beginning, of course, of thinking about it. Having Short Views read aloud also allows the instructor to see which ones create a response from the class, a question, a look of puzzlement, a laugh, or a groan. Any one of these responses is a good place to start discussion. "What is it here that makes you laugh?" Or, "Is there something here you don't understand? Or are you saying you disagree? Try to slow down your reaction and see if you can explain it."

Sometimes we write a Short View on the blackboard to demonstrate what we mean by analysis of a written text.

Take, for example, Vince Lombardi's "Winning is not the most important thing; it's everything" (*LBR*, p. 387). We might start by asking "Who is (was) Vince Lombardi?" Many students will know that he coached the Green Bay Packers, that they won the first two Super Bowls in the 1960s, and that the Super Bowl trophy is called the Vince Lombardi Trophy. They'll know a lot more, but for now, this is enough exposition (the background that helps to identify and explain the text). Now, what does it mean, to start with, "Winning is not the most important thing?" Who said that it was? This is a bit puzzling because it isn't something that's usually said; it is, rather, assumed. Assumptions, unlike assertions, are often unspoken because the speaker thinks that everyone is in agreement or thinks the point is obvious, and perhaps does not even realize that the assumption is part of his or her own reasoning. When Lombardi says, "Winning is not the most important thing," we think at first that he is arguing against this assumption. But of course he is not, as we find out almost immediately with "it's everything." The first part of his message is, then, ironic. He means almost the opposite of what he appears to mean.

But there is a subtext here. As soon as we hear "Winning isn't the most important thing," we expect to hear "it's how you play the game." What, then is Lombardi implying? (An implication is what follows from an assertion or an argument.) Is he implying that sportsmanship doesn't matter? Or that team play doesn't? Or being a good loser? Or doing your personal best? How would you characterize Lombardi's tone here? And do you agree with him that winning is "everything" or not?

Other suggestions for using Short Views occur throughout this manual.

1

---◆◆◆---

A WRITER READS

J. H. Plumb
The Dying Family (p. 6)

Instructors who have read our discussions of skimming, highlighting, outlining, and so on in Chapter 1 will not want us to go into additional detail about these topics. But a few remarks about some of Plumb's methods in this essay may be useful.

Plumb begins nicely with a specific, dramatic illustration, the episode (we are almost led to believe) that inspired his reflections. And it provides a framework, for at the end of his essay Plumb will refer to "that bus load of children. . . ." Note, too, that Plumb begins with "I," a word many students needlessly fear to use.

The whole essay is admirably concrete. For example, the third paragraph tells us not that the family has fulfilled "several" functions but that it has fulfilled "three social functions." And it doesn't simply say that in the peasant world, children of four and five could earn their keep, for Plumb goes on to add, "as they still can in India and Africa." Similarly, in the next paragraph he glosses "very primitive people who live in a pre-agrarian society" with "as with the Esquimaux."

The assertion that the Eskimo (to use the more common spelling) are a "primitive people"—more exactly, that "people who live in a pre-agrarian society" are "primitive"—may well be found offensive by some students, and on the whole we agree that it is. The word "primitive" (derived ultimately from the Latin *primus*, "first") was widely used by anthropologists in the late nineteenth and early twentieth centuries to indicate a society that supposedly was still in the first stage of an evolutionary process that culminated in "civilization," whose finest flowering was a white industrial society. Today virtually all anthropologists agree that the word "primitive" is at best misleading, not only because it implies that the products of a "primitive" society (art, myths, etc.) are crude but also because it implies that such a society does not itself have a long history.

Topics for Critical Thinking and Writing

1. In his concluding paragraph Plumb refers to "the revolution in eating" as evidence of the decline of the family. Think about the eating habits of a family or families that you know well. What do those habits or patterns tell you about the strength of family life? You might want to consider some of the following questions: Do members of the family regularly eat together at home? Do they eat food prepared at home or do they rely heavily on "take-out" fast food or frozen microwavable packages? Do they enjoy traditional foods that reflect their ethnic heritage? If they eat in restaurants, do they do so together, as a family? Do family members converse during meals, exchanging news, advice, or jokes? Or do

they watch television while they eat, or listen to music, or read? Are guests frequent or infrequent? These questions are suggestions only for discovering patterns of family eating, and you need not consider them. But try to make your discussion specific, by looking at a specific family or families, and then explain what conclusions you draw about the relationship of eating habits and the strength of family life or the strains on it.

2. What support would Plumb's essay offer the anonymous author of "Confessions of an Erstwhile Child" *(LBR)*?

3. Question 3, Chapter 6, following Coser's essay calls for a comparison of Plumb and Coser.

2

---◆·◆·◆---

A READER WRITES

C. S. Lewis
We Have No "Right to Happiness" (p. 20)

Because the essay is examined at considerable length in the text, some instructors may not wish to devote class time to a further discussion of it. On the other hand, it does go over very well in class, and the comments in the text by no means exhaust it. One point is especially provocative: the reasons Lewis offers (in his next-to-last paragraph) for the greater vulnerability of women—that they are "more naturally monogamous than men," and that, unlike men, they care less about "looks" in their partners than about personality—antagonize some students (roughly half of the class). We find ourselves conceding that Lewis, who wrote the essay in 1963, would almost certainly have modulated his language were he writing today. Note, for example, his pronouns (emphasis added) in "domestic happiness is more necessary to *them* than to *us*." But we doubt that he would have altered his ideas because, in our opinion, they still hold. Without attempting to impose our own ideas, or for that matter Lewis's, on the class, we ask them to consider what for most young students is a novelty, and for all of us a burden: that an idea can be displeasing and still be true.

Topics for Critical Thinking and Writing

1. Do you agree with Lewis's statement (paragraph 6) that "we depend for a very great deal of our happiness or misery on circumstances outside all human control"?

2. What specific moral obligations do you acknowledge? How did you acquire your sense of obligation? How would you argue their claims to someone who did not acknowledge them?

3. Lewis says that "Our sexual impulses are . . . being put in a position of preposterous privilege." Explain what he means and whether you agree with him.

4. How, according to Lewis, does sexual infidelity ultimately threaten civilization?

5. Write a reply to Lewis's essay, from Clare's point of view, or from Mr. A's.

3

---◆◆◆---

ACADEMIC WRITING

More about Critical Thinking

At the end of our discussion of Notman's photograph of Sitting Bull and Buffalo Bill, we suggest that students may be stimulated to critical thinking if they compare the 1911 account of Sitting Bull in the *Encyclopedia Britannica* (11th edition) with the account in the latest *Britannica*. For convenience we reproduce the 1911 account here.

> **SITTING BULL** (*c.* 1837–1890), a chief and medicine man of the Dakota Sioux, was born on Willow Creek in what is now North Dakota about 1837, son of a chief named Jumping Bull. He gained great influence among the reckless and unruly young Indians, and during the Civil War led attacks on white settlements in Iowa and Minnesota. Though he had pretended to make peace in 1866, from 1869 to 1876 he frequently attacked whites or Indians friendly to whites. His refusal to return to the reservation in 1876 led to the campaign in which General George A. Custer (*q.v.*) and his command were massacred. Fearing punishment for his participation in the massacre, Sitting Bull with a large band moved over into Canada. He returned to the United States in 1881, and after 1883 made his home at the Standing Rock Agency. Rumours of a coming Indian Messiah who should sweep away the whites, and Indian dissatisfaction at the sale of their lands, created such great unrest in Dakota in 1889–1890 that it was determined to arrest Sitting Bull as a precaution. He was surprised and captured by Indian police and soldiers on Grand river on the 15th of December 1890, and was killed while his companions were attempting to rescue him.

We do not reproduce the latest version, since whatever we reproduce may be superseded by the time this manual is published, but we are confident that it presents Sitting Bull in a more favorable light. Thus, it will not include such sentences as these, from the preceding account:

- "He gained great influence among the reckless and unruly young Indians. . . ."
- "Though he had pretended to make peace . . . , he frequently attacked whites or Indians friendly to whites."
- "His refusal to return to the reservation in 1876 led to the campaign in which General George A. Custer (*q.v.*) and his command were massacred."

On the contrary, modern accounts emphasize the injustices inflicted on the Indians by whites and the leadership skills of Sitting Bull. Whereas earlier writers instructed their readers that Indians massacred whites, and whites "subdued" Indians, today's writers are likely to instruct their readers that whites massacred Indians, and that the Indians were forced to fight for their survival. Thus, the 1993 *Britannica* says of Sitting Bull, "He was in frequent hostile contact with the army, which was invading the Sioux hunting grounds and bringing ruin to the Indian economy." The 1993 version admits that in 1875–1876 Sitting Bull refused to return to the reservation, but it plausibly adds that "even had Sitting Bull been willing to comply, he could not possibly have moved his village 340 miles (390km) in the bitter cold by the specified time."

You may want to use this particular exercise, by the way, as a transition to the next chapter, "Writing an Argument," because the exercise can be used as a way to guide students to scrutinize assumptions and especially to look for *unstated* assumptions.

A Note on Academic Prose

Students unaccountably persist—even after we tell them not to—in "writing for the teacher." Maybe they know something we don't know.

Still, we think we are right in telling them that (in the absence of instructions to the contrary) when they write papers in college courses they should assume their audience to be their classmates. Of course an "academic" audience may be more specialized: they may on occasion be writing, for instance, to the dean, or to a faculty committee, and in the course of their years in the college—even in their very first semester—they will encounter a range of academic writings. They should keep their eyes and ears open, reading attentively, noticing the differences in the kinds of writings they encounter.

What advice can we suggest that instructors offer to students? Perhaps the best advice any instructor can offer is this:

Follow the guidelines that the instructor sets concerning
- Length
- System of documentation
- Date due
- Format, including whether to use a staple, a paper clip, or no fastener at all

Oh yes, one more thing:
- Be sure to spell the instructor's name correctly.

The chapter emphasizes the perhaps obvious point that most academic writing is analytic, and it seeks to illustrate analysis by examining a photograph of Sitting Bull and Buffalo Bill. You may well want to ask the students to analyze another picture, either a picture in this book or in a current news magazine.

Mark Edmundson
How Teachers Can Stop Cheaters (p. 68)

We include this short essay in our chapter on academic writing because it raises the issue of plagiarism, but the cheating that Edmundson is talking about is the wholesale use of purchased papers rather than the improper citation of sources. You may, therefore, want to to teach Edmundson's essay in connection with Chapter 8, "Teaching and Learning," possibly in connection with Stanley Fish's essay, "Why We Built the Ivory Tower," or possibly even in connection with the casebook on examinations, i.e., in a context that asks, "What is the point of written assignments?"

Possibly we are living in an ivory tower, but it is our impression that very few of our students have submitted papers that were either bought or lifted from some published source, and our explanation is simple: The topics we assign are usually very specific. That is, we don't assign such topics as "Do you think tests are useful in English courses?" or (in a literature course) "Compare two characters in *Macbeth*." Rather, we give, for instance, two opposing quotations from essays in *LBR* and ask the students to evaluate and comment on these assertions. Or, again beginning with a quotation from a work in the text, we might ask students to imagine how some other author represented in the book would reply to it.

Of course, it is possible that a friend writes the paper for the student, or maybe the student even commissions an Internet source to write the paper, but we are fairly confident that assignments of this type greatly diminish the chance that a paper is not the student's own work.

As for Edmundson's essay, we don't have much to add. We agree that English teachers are chiefly concerned with teaching close reading—which largely means that teachers in a composition course are teaching students how to read their *own* works closely, i.e., we are largely teaching the art of *revising*. But we also agree with Edmundson that the teaching of the analysis of language "is not nearly enough." Edmundson goes on to say that when we teach literature—but surely he would also include essays of the sort that constitute most of *LBR*—"We need to go further and ask if those works provide usable truths for ourselves and our students." Discuss.

4

WRITING AN ARGUMENT

Richard Rhodes
Hollow Claims about Fantasy Violence (p. 91)

Because we discuss the rhetoric of this essay at length in the text, there is no need to talk about this aspect here, but a brief comment on the central issue may be appropriate. It is our impression, partly based on responses in the classroom, that many people—we are tempted to say "most students"—believe that studies have proven that violence in the media leads to violence in real life. Probably a chief cause of this belief is the occasional *Time* magazine report that some nut says he killed because he saw such a killing in a film or read about it in a comic book. A second cause is that critics of the media seem to make good witnesses at congressional hearings on the issue.

In fact, however—we think it is a fact—a majority of studies of the issue take the contrary view, or at least they suggest there is little evidence that media violence (Rhodes's "mock violence") causes real violence. What does seem to be demonstrated is that persons who are unusually aggressive are also persons who especially delight in media violence, who look at a lot of it, who play violent games, etc. But, obviously, such a correlation does *not* mean that media violence *causes* normal people to act violently.

As we see it, opposed to the people who claim that the media cause violence are (speaking a bit broadly) people who are devoted to cultural studies. The cultural studies folk tend to argue that (a) the media do not cause violence in normal viewers, and (b) the media in fact have a wholesome effect, since the violence that they portray serves as a sort of safety valve, allowing normal viewers to vent their violent feelings harmlessly—the old idea of catharsis.

For a very readable short book on this last point, see Jib Fowles, *The Case for Television Violence* (1999). For a variety of points of view, see *From Barbie to Mortal Kombat: Gender and Computer Games*, ed. Henry Jenkins and Justine Cassell (1998).

Gary Shapiro
Lasting Impression—Downloading Is Illegal (p. 97)

Perhaps the first thing to note about Gary Shapiro's essay is that its author isn't exactly a disinterested party (people who write arguments generally aren't, of course). As President and CEO of the Consumer Electronics Association, he represents companies that, among other things, make the devices on which downloaded music may be played. He uses several strategies to persuade readers to his point of view and to present himself as reasonable and authoritative. He presents his thesis clearly and emphatically in paragraph 2: "The pervasive theme of copyspeak is that downloading from the Internet is both illegal and immoral. It is neither." He immediately acknowledges that the counterargument has some merit, thus presenting himself as a fair-minded thinker, someone we can trust. He notes that "there is little doubt that some use the benefits of technology to make and distribute unauthorized copies for personal financial gain in clear violation of copyright law." Then, in paragraph 3, he presents the alarming claim—a claim that he does not support with evidence—that "if the play button becomes the pay button, our very ability to raise the world's standard of living and education will be jeopardized." (His argument would be more compelling, we think, if he were to point to particular effects on education and economics.)

His tone combines mild scorn for his opponents, who indulge in what he calls "copyspeak," and a world-weary exasperation with their foolish claims: "we've been down [this] road . . . before." (In general, in writing an argument it is not a good idea to express scorn or impatience; your readers are more likely to be persuaded if they sense that you are well meaning and thoughtful, not a wiseguy.) Wanting to set us straight, Shapiro advises us "to take a close, hard look" at the idea that downloading—which, according to his statistics, "most Americans between 13 and 25 engage in regularly"—is criminal.

A first step is defining a key term in his argument: "Fair use rights—the right of consumers to make copies of copyrighted materials for their personal use—are guaranteed to consumers by statute, and applied judicially on a case-by-case basis."

He also presents analogies. He compares downloading music and taping movies on VCRs (which was declared legal by the Supreme Court in the Betamax case of 1984, in which the film industry sued Sony for making it possible for consumers to videotape movies). He also draws an analogy between real property and coyrighted intellectual property. The latter, he claims, is an analogy that "fails": downloading is justifiable precisely because copyrighted material is not analogous to real property, which can be owned forever.

In his response to Shapiro's argument, Cary Sherman will take particular issue with this definition of "fair use rights" and with the claims about property.

Cary Sherman
Perspective: Honest Talk about Downloads (p. 100)

Like Shapiro, Sherman is no disinterested participant in this debate. As president of the Recording Industry Association of America, he represents the recording industry, which claims to be losing a great deal of money because of illegal downloading. In paragraph 18 of his essay, Shapiro presents statistics to support this claim and to contest Shapiro's assertion that the recording industry is doing just fine. He notes a 10 percent decline in the sales of recorded music in 2001 and an additional 10 percent decline in the first half of 2002. He also presents evidence from authority to support his claim that Shapiro is simply *wrong*: unauthorized downloading is illegal because of "Title 17 of the United States Code, which prohibits the unauthorized reproduction, distribution, or digital transmission of copyrighted material," not because of "assertions of the Justice Department"—a phrase that now looks vague and imprecise.

The heart of Sherman's argument is his analysis of Shapiro's claims about music, property, and fair use rights. In paragraph 6, Sherman complains that Shapiro doesn't set out exactly what these rights are. Sherman himself doesn't define these rights either, except to say that they don't "justify the uploading and downloading between anonymous strangers of entire copyrighted works of entertainment." In paragraph 9, he calls into question Shapiro's analogy between home recording of films ("the Betamax case"), again by presenting evidence from authority. The courts, he says, have not found a similarity between downloading and home video recording. In paragraphs 12 and 13, Sherman asserts that stealing a dress and downloading a piece of music, are, in fact, analogous (Shapiro had offered this analogy, only to dispute it).

Sherman's tone is by turns angry, sarcastic, witty, and reasonable. In our comment on Shapiro's essay, we cautioned against expressing scorn or impatience. On the other hand, if you are writing about something that strikes you as morally outrageous, of course you may convey anger, not sweet reasonableness. In paragraph 2, Sherman calls Shapiro's argument "specious" and says that if it isn't "a deliberate and outright attempt to misinform" then it's "at best . . . wishful thinking." Later, in paragraph 16, he uses sarcasm as he draws an analogy between downloading and plagiarism: "Plagiarists, take heart: Stealing other people's writing is OK with Shapiro, just as long as you don't steal the computer they wrote it on"

Sherman turns to wit when he criticizes Shapiro's "portrait of artists as crybaby Luddites" (the shift in diction, the informal "crybaby" modifying the word "Luddite", a term from a very different level of usage, is funny). But he also presents himself as a reasonable person: in paragraph 3, he acknowledges the counterargument when he notes that "there is nothing wrong with downloading per se"; he does this again in paragraph 7 when he grants that "we all respect and support fair use," and again in the final sentence of the essay when he presents himself as interested in finding ways "to better serve consumers, creators, and technology companies."

5

———◆◆◆———

READING AND WRITING
ABOUT PICTURES

Lou Jacobs Jr.
What Qualities Does a Good Photograph Have? (p. 112)

Although the first word of Jacobs's first paragraph might have been "None," the title leads a reader to expect that Jacobs will indeed name some qualities, and he does. He believes there are "criteria" (paragraph 2) for judging photographs (works of art, we might say), although in paragraph 4 he grants that judging photographs includes a "subjective" element. His compromise position is that "there is enough agreement in the tastes of a variety of people to make certain standards general and valid" (paragraph 4).

Jacobs is not a philosopher trying to set forth an airtight case in *Journal of Aesthetics and Art Criticism,* and it would be inappropriate to press him very hard concerning the meaning of key terms, such as *enough agreement, taste, general,* and *valid.* His words are clear enough to ordinary readers, and they make considerable sense. Most of us probably are of two minds when it comes to matters of aesthetic judgment: with half of our mind we say *De gustibus non est diputandum*—well, we probably say it in English, "There's no disputing about tastes"—and with the other half we say, "Of course I know what is good and what is bad. What is more, I can explain why this movie is better than that, or this novel is better than that." If we recommend a movie to a friend and then she tells us that she didn't care for it at all, we are likely to say things like, "What didn't you like about it?" and "Didn't you think the characters were interesting, and weren't the settings beautiful? And the dialogue! It was so witty!" That is, we do *not* assume that a film (or a play, or—can we say a photograph?) is like a dish of ice cream. If someone says she prefers vanilla to chocolate, we *don't* ask her why she has this preference. We assume, in this instance, that there is no disputing tastes. But, again, with works of art (films, photographs, novels, etc.) most of us do try to give reasons for our responses, which implies that there are standards. These standards may not be universal (probably few people think that African sculpture, Impressionist painting, and American Indian beadwork can all be judged by the same criteria); they may be limited to what has recently been called an interpretive community. Half a dozen teachers of composition may disagree about which essay (out of a hundred) gets first prize in an essay competition, but they will probably agree, with very few exceptions, about which five essays are the strongest candidates for first prize, and they will also agree about which essays are in the top quarter and about which are in the bottom quarter. Similarly, a panel of judges at a photography exhibition will share most values and will agree in their evaluations of most of the works in the exhibition. Different final judgments will often boil down to differences in the weight allotted to one criterion or another—just as they usually do in evaluating figure skating, automobiles, candidates for admission to college or to graduate school, and candidates for jobs.

So much by way of background. In teaching Jacobs's essay, you may want to ask students if, given the limitations of space, Jacobs has made clear his criteria. If more space had been available, doubtless he would have included two images for each criterion, one image showing a photograph lacking in the quality under discussion (say, "human interest"), the other showing a photograph strong in this quality. Our own feeling is that Jacobs is pretty vague about his first quality, "impact," but pretty clear about the others.

Topics for Critical Thinking and Writing

1. If you think Jacobs omits some important criteria, write a response (350–500 words) to his essay.

2. If you think that it is impossible to evaluate rationally the qualities of photographs, set forth your reasons in an essay of 250 words.

3. Suppose someone were to say to you that Ansel Adams's *Moonrise, Hernandez, NM,* with its small glowing crosses in a vast landscape is a sentimental picture and therefore not of high quality. What would be your written response?

4. If you think Jacobs makes sense, discuss two of the pictures in *The Little, Brown Reader,* using some or all of his criteria.

Joan Daremo
Edvard Munch's *The Scream* (p. 117)

Daremo's essay seems to us to be a good example of a formal analysis of a picture. It was written by an undergraduate who had elected a course in art history, so we can't say it is representative of the work that any first-year student might do in a composition course, but in fact we have had excellent essays in our introductory composition courses. Why? Our tentative answer is that students can write very well when they keep their eye on an object. If they look closely and ask themselves questions (e.g., What is the effect of this figure? Of lines of this sort?), they will find they can produce responses that will interest them and their readers.

The Scream, like Grant Wood's *American Gothic,* Michelangelo's *David,* and several paintings by van Gogh—and maybe *Whistler's Mother*—must be one of the very few works of art that almost every student will know. And, like *American Gothic,* it has produced parodies of various sorts, e.g., an election button that showed the image, with the word "President" at the top and the word "Quayle" at the bottom. Also available, according to a few minutes that we spent on the Internet: *The Scream* posters, mouse pads, neckties, ceramics, pillows, and switchplates.

Zoe Morales
Dancing at Durango: White Tourists and Navajo Performers (p. 119)

First, we should mention why, when we assign students to write about a picture, we distribute the picture or several pictures, rather than giving students their choice of any picture. It turns out that many Internet services maintain a stock of essays on famous pictures—works of art and well-known contemporary advertisements—which they offer for sale supposedly as an aid to the student, but in fact some students are tempted to submit the purchased paper. Because we prefer not to make an assignment that puts temptation in the student's path, we provide images that almost certainly are not the subjects of Internet "aids."

When we assign Morales's essay we urge the students to study Morales's preliminary notes—really her final notes—so that they will see that even a good set of notes will undergo plenty of revision when they are turned into a good paper. Here is our overview of Morales's essay.

- The title of the essay is not simply "An analysis . . ."; rather, the title arouses interest.
- The essay includes some *description* ("The train has stopped, some people have stepped off," the train "uses a style of lettering that looks like a Wanted Poster"), but, more important, it includes *analysis*. That is, it sees how these elements work to make a meaningful whole. Thus, when Zoe Morales tells us that the photo shows a man and boy who have stepped off the train, she is being descriptive, but when she goes on to say that they wear clothing that makes them clearly distinguishable from the other characters on the ground, she is being analytic. Similarly, the statement that the train is labeled with lettering of the Wanted Poster sort is a descriptive statement, but the statement that this lettering is meant to suggest a romantic past is analytic.
- Formal analysis dominates the third and fourth paragraphs, but the essay also includes the writer's reflections on the image, especially in the final paragraph.

A topic for class discussion: What grade would you give Morales's essay? Why?

Jason Green

Did Dorothea Lange Pose Her Subject for *Migrant Mother*? (p. 124)

Lange worked for the Historical Section of Franklin D. Roosevelt's newly formed Resettlement Administration, a body charged with getting financial aid to dispossessed farmworkers. (It was later incorporated into the Farm Security Administration.) The photographic division was essentially a public relations agency whose job was to give pictures, at no charge, to newspapers and magazines, in an effort to publicize Roosevelt's New Deal. After Lange took *Migrant Mother,* she gave the picture (and some others of the same subject) to an editor at the *San Francisco News,* and she told him that the pea pickers were starving. He alerted the United Press, which in turn contacted relief authorities who sent food to the camp.

Lange was known for her compassion—the photographs themselves seem to establish the matter beyond all doubt—and she was also known for her (relatively) hands-off approach to photography. Here is one of her statements about her methods:

> My own approach is based upon three considerations. First—hands off! Whatever I photograph, I do not molest or tamper with or arrange. Second—a sense of place. Whatever I photograph, I try to picture as part of its surroundings, as having roots. Third—sense of time. Whatever I photograph, I try to show as having its position in the past or in the present.
>
> Quoted in Daniel Dixon, "Dorothea Lange,"
> *Modern Photography* 16 (December 1952): 68

Of course, "Hands off" is a relative term. If you take a picture of someone, are you really keeping your hands off them? (Student-photographers may well write forcefully on this topic.) Further, Lange composed the scenes at least to the extent that she had to choose the distance and the angle. Lange's second point, about the sense of place, is interesting in connection with *Migrant Mother* precisely because the picture does not give a sense of place. The other pictures that Lange took of the same subject show the woman in a context (sitting in a crude shelter, made of cloth hanging from a pole, with some landscape visible at the right). These other pictures are moving, but not nearly so much as the famous picture.

Topics for Critical Thinking and Writing

1. Do photographers have a moral right to take pictures of unfortunate persons (e.g., a sleeping homeless family or a despondent unemployed person) without the consent of the subjects? (You may want to locate such a photo in a weekly

newsmagazine and base your essay on it. Hand in a photocopy of the picture with your essay.)

2. *A research paper:* In the 1930s, Lange worked for the Resettlement Administration (later incorporated into the Farm Security Administration), an agency established as part of Franklin D. Roosevelt's New Deal. What were the aims and functions of the photographers who worked for this agency? (Books and essays on Lange are good places to begin. If your library has a book by Roy E. Stryker—chief of the photographic division—you may want to start there.)

6

ALL IN THE FAMILY

Illustrations

Joanne Leonard
Sonia (p. 136)

This picture, apparently a snapshot, is close in feel to many of Cartier-Bresson's well-known photographs: beauty shines through the commonplace. At this moment everything is just right: the profile of the woman fully reveals her pregnancy, as does the transparent garment. She is caught in a moment of domestic work, and we can easily foresee the increased domestic work ahead, especially the laundering of clothing. The natural process in her womb has an affinity with the growing grass and flowers. The scene is, in a way, lyrical and pastoral, but the crude fence and the ropes keep the scene well on this side of sentimentality.

Some photographers have implied that pictures like Cartier-Bresson's Old World scenes are impossible in America, where billboards and asphalt highways mar the landscape and where neon signs and rubbish mar the streets. But Leonard has managed to catch beauty in a backyard.

Pablo Picasso
The Acrobat's Family with a Monkey (p. 137)

The Acrobat's Family with a Monkey is an early painting, done just after Picasso's "blue" period of 1903–1904, which was characterized by mannered, elongated figures in awkward postures. Around 1905 Picasso turned to circus motifs, doubtless seeing in Harlequin an image of the artist as an outsider who possessed a skill or discipline that the slovenly bourgeois world neglected. The artist, like Harlequin, does not share in the riches (or even in the clothing) of the materialistic world, but he is sustained by the dignity that skill confers.

In this painting there is still some of the elongation of the figures of the blue period, and the consequent implication of hunger, but there is also—in place of the pathetic and sometimes bathetic loneliness of those pictures—a sense of domestic tenderness. The baby may grow into an emaciated, melancholy harlequin, but for the moment he is pleasantly chubby and a source of grave pleasure. The monkey plays his part too, for the animal serves to accentuate the ties that bind the human family but separate the family from the lower creatures; the monkey seems to be trying to enter the world of the family, but it is ignored. (Notice, however, that compared to the mother, the father is outside the infant's world. The infant touches the mother but not the father.)

Inevitably the picture evokes, at least at the fringes of our minds, pictures of the Holy Family. The animal plays a part here too, for pictures of the Holy Family often include a beast—usually a lamb but, in an engraving by Dürer, a monkey.

Short Views

Topics for Critical Thinking and Writing

1. Describe a person you know who illustrates Proust's remark.

2. Suppose that we transform Proust's remark to "Up to a certain age, the more one becomes oneself, the less one resembles one's parents." Argue the point.

3. We can transform Tolstoy's quotation to "All unhappy families resemble one another; every happy family is happy in its own fashion." Explain, and defend by the use of examples.

4. Argue the special difficulties (or advantages) of being an only child (or the oldest child, or a middle child, or the youngest child).

Here are some additional short reviews that you may want to discuss with your students.

1. Man is the head of the family, woman the neck that turns the head.
   Chinese aphorism
   (If you have any Chinese or Chinese-American students, ask them if this sounds true, and then invite other students to their views.)

2. Men are from Mars, women from Venus.
   Anonymous

3. Marriage is for women the commonest mode of livelihood, and the total amount of undesired sex endured by women is probably greater in marriage than in prostitution.
   Bertrand Russell, writing in 1929 (in *Marriage and Morals*)

Lewis Coser
The Family (p. 140)

In his first sentence Coser speaks of the "nuclear" family; when assigning the selection it is useful to ask students to look up the etymology of this word and to think about its metaphoric application. ("Nuclear" is from the Latin *nucleus* = nut, kernel.) In biology the word refers to a complex within a living cell that contains the cell's hereditary material and that controls its metabolism, growth, and reproduction. A dictionary will also cite meanings in botany, anatomy, and physics; it is our impression that sociologists have adopted the word in an effort to acquire the prestige of the sciences. In any case, we can't quite see that the "nuclear family" means anything more than a family consisting of parents and their children; it does not, for example, retain the idea that this nucleus is the center of a larger unit.

It is not Coser's fault, of course, that sociology uses the term "nuclear family." Nor is it his fault that students may not know the meanings of such words as *matrilocal* or *neolocal* and *endogamous* or *exogamous*. This short essay provides a chance to talk about the distinction between appropriate technical language and jargon: the distinction between words that, to an initiated audience, are precise and words that are used perhaps to impress or even to mystify an uninitiated audience. It also provides an opportunity to mention the differences between disciplines. Each academic discipline has special terms and definitions for those terms. To learn to write in different disciplines one must learn what the terms mean in that discipline and how they are used.

Coser's writing is not entirely free from inflated sociologese. We can't understand why he prefers "manifesting" to "showing" and "erroneous" to "false" or "mistaken." Still, his essay seems to us to be fairly good prose of its sort, although it is not the sort we read for pleasure. If students are invited to say what they find difficult about it, they will come to see the importance of using nontechnical language when writing for a general audience, as well as the importance of giving concrete examples. Although concrete examples are not needed here to clarify the points, they would make the piece more interesting.

Topics for Critical Thinking and Writing

Coser assumes, properly enough, an audience familiar with the language of sociology. It can be useful to ask students to rewrite his third paragraph for, say, a high school audience. Also, the third question in the text can be answered in a brief essay. Students might be invited to amplify their answers with examples from their own experiences.

Francis Bacon
Of Marriage and Single Life (p. 141)

Although first-year students find this essay difficult to understand, we think there is value in spending class time on it, paying attention not only to

Bacon's ideas but also to his style. That's why in our first question we ask students to paraphrase a sentence, and we ask them in our third question to begin a sentence with "Husbands are," and to continue it with an imitation of Bacon's "Wives are young men's mistresses, companions for middle age, and old men's nurses."

The point is to help students to see that sentences must have shape and that the shape helps to convey—or embody—the meaning. Bacon teaches students nothing about the overall organization of the essay—his essay is chiefly a loose assemblage of arresting thoughts—but he can teach them a great deal about the sound and shape of an effective sentence. And a good way to get his learning into their bones is to have them write imitations of some of his sentences.

Additional Suggestion for Writing

Imitating Bacon's style, write a caption for one of the illustrations in *LBR*. Here are some examples from our students:

a. For "Sonia" (p. 136): "A woman who enjoys her work and her body is beautiful to behold." Also: "If men did the laundry, there would be fewer babies."
b. For "Children" (p. 385): "The mask that a child playfully puts on, he will soon put on in earnest." Also: "Children wear masks in play, adults wear masks in earnest."

Joan Didion
On Going Home (p. 143)

In a typical freshman English class, made up of seventeen- to nineteen-year-olds, some students reading Didion will find her style heady and her topic compelling for their own writing. Others will be irritated, some without knowing why. Still others will be indifferent. Typically, whatever their intellectual range, students at this age vary markedly in emotional maturity. Some, we find, are not ready for the confrontation with their own ambivalence toward their families that a serious engagement with Didion's essay demands. So, although we would assign the essay and discuss it in class, we wouldn't *require* essays written about it. We don't want to read the vague or sentimental essays some would submit; and with so much else to write about, there's no reason to put students on a collision course with failure. For students who can and will use them, the questions following the piece provide some sample essay topics.

Gabrielle Glaser
Scenes from an Intermarriage (p. 146)

Most students have not heard of or seen Ingmar Bergman's television series "Scenes from a Marriage," but they might be interested in learning that it exists, and one can ask whether or not "Scenes from an Intermarriage," which alludes to it, is an effective title for this essay. We think that it is; Glaser for the most part avoids judgments and pronouncements by showing us the decoration of the Ono house and the family discussing their religious observances, their celebration of holidays, the Ono wedding. The scenes reveal the compromises the Onos (particularly Eileen) have made and, generally, the success of their decision to raise the children as Buddhists.

We include interracial as well as interfaith marriages in our class discussion and encourage students to write on interracial relationships if they choose. We refer to the paragraph in which Glaser reveals that Sarah and Alistair were "taunted . . . on the playground" and Alistair's rebuke from an English teacher (paragraph 18) and invite discussion from students about parallel experiences in their lives.

Anonymous
Confessions of an Erstwhile Child (p. 151)

When we discuss this anonymous essay in class, we usually analyze the opening paragraph in detail (calling attention to the leisurely, informal initial phrase, the abruptness of the first clause of the second sentence, the neat summaries in the third and fourth sentences, and so on), and then we go on to talk about the organization of the beginning. After all, the essay might have begun with the second paragraph ("The idea of the child as property"); we try, then, to get students to see what the earlier paragraphs do.

We try, also, to remind students that the writer of a persuasive essay must somehow convince readers of his or her competence and honesty; the anonymous author of "Confessions" does this partly by assuring us that he speaks from experience and partly by admitting his defects ("I am a very cold-hearted man"). Then, too, he gains our sympathy by presenting himself as a victim, and he holds our sympathy by assuring us that he knows other people have been equally victimized ("I survived because statistically most people 'survive' horrible families"). Furthermore, he helps to convince us of his clear-headedness and of the sanity of his unusual proposal by telling us, at the beginning of the last paragraph, that "the risk of rackets [under his proposal] would be very high"; that is, he recognizes the weakness and thereby neatly prevents us from labeling the proposal as utopian nonsense.

The chief difficulty with discussing the essay as a piece of persuasive writing is that it comes so close to the bone, or the heart, that students can scarcely be restrained from getting off into arguments about the issue at stake. The difficulty can be exploited by channeling the discussion into writing assignments. Questions 2 and 4 provide additional topics for writing. Note also that the second question for writing following our discussion of Plumb (manual, p. 14) calls for a comparison with "Confessions."

Note: John Holt, in *Escape from Childhood* (1974), discusses children's rights extensively. He argues not only that children should have the right to choose their guardians (the point Anonymous makes), but also that they should have "the right to do, in general, what any adult may legally do."

Julie Matthaei
Political Economy and Family Policy (p. 156)

As with most essays, one can begin class discussion of "Political Economy and Family Policy" by asking questions about the essay's content, or one can begin with a comment on the essay's form and style. With such provocative content, we wouldn't know how to head off discussion of it if we wanted to, so we start there.

Although the essay is admirably clear and almost jargon-free, almost every sentence is dense with implications or assumptions that might go unnoticed unless questioned. Here are four such sentences and some questions we ask about them.

1. In the first sentence (of paragraph 1, after the Abstract), Matthaei claims that the family plays a central role in "reproducing class, race, and gender inequalities." Assuming that there are such inequalities (and most of us are willing to grant that there are), how does the family, according to Matthaei, reproduce inequalities? Does the essay explain and support the claim that it does? (See paragraphs 8–11.) What other explanations have been offered for inequalities between, for example, genders? (You may want to assign Stephen Gould's "Women's Brains.") Does Matthaei assume that all inequalities are socially created? Does she assume that all or most inequalities can be eliminated? By what means? (See paragraphs 13 to end.)
2. In paragraph 22 (last sentence), Matthaei admits that the new family system she advocates "may appear utopian" but "many are living out parts of this vision now." What does "utopian" mean in this sentence? Paragraphs 23 and 24 define "social marriage" and "social parenting." Do they appear utopian? From your own experience, do you agree that "many are living out parts of this vision now"?

3. In paragraph 23, describing "social marriage," Matthaei says (in the last sentence) that couples would not need to stay together "'for better or for worse . . . as long as ye both shall live' . . . since each would have earnings." What is her assumption here? Do you share it? What reasons other than economic might a couple have for staying together "for better or worse"?

4. In paragraph 28, third sentence, Matthaei argues that "society must recognize the right of those who are infertile, gay, or single to parent. . . ." What is the basis of this right? Might a right to parent be construed from the right to "the pursuit of happiness"? And what, by the way, gives us that right? (See C. S. Lewis, "We Have No 'Right to Happiness.'") How might this right conflict with the best interests of a child?

A word on the form and style of the essay. We find Matthaei's piece forcefully written and, although more radical than most of the material students will encounter in their courses, a good example of writing in the social sciences. We note, for example, the abstract of the argument, the series of subtitles in boldface (that let readers thread their way through the argument almost effortlessly), the announced purpose of the essay in the second sentence, and the informative endnotes.

Katharine Graham
On Money, Religion, and Sex (p. 168)

Graham led an extraordinary life—as daughter, wife, widow, and independent woman. Leafing through pages of her memoir, *Personal History,* one finds photographs of her parents taken by Edward Steichen, of the splendid family houses in Washington, D.C., and Mount Kisco, of her husband on the cover of *Time,* and of Katharine, after her widowhood, with President Johnson, Bobby Kennedy, Vice President Nixon, Henry Kissinger, Indira Gandhi, the Prince and Princess of Wales, President and Mrs. Reagan, President Clinton, and many others. James Reston was a close personal friend; she dated Adlai Stevenson. She steered the *Washington Post* through the crises of the Pentagon Papers and Watergate. And her memoir, which she wrote without a co-author, won a Pulitzer Prize. Reading it, though, while aware of Graham's importance and prestige, one feels comfortable; her writing is candid, unpretentious, and often very amusing. We hope that students reading this brief excerpt can sense these qualities of her style and that many will want to read the entire memoir.

Money, religion, and sex, and how one's parents dealt with them, strike us as appealing topics for students to write about. We suggest an essay topic following our third question in the text. Questions 1 and 4 can also provide essay topics.

Arlie Hochschild
The Second Shift: Employed Women Are Putting in Another Day of Work at Home (p. 172)

Hochschild defines in his first paragraph what he means by the "economic and cultural trends" that affect American families: inflation, an expanding service sector, which has opened jobs for women, and the "inroads made by women into many professions." The article was written over fifteen years ago, and many students are unaware that there have been both new opportunities for women in the workforce and a greater need by many families for two incomes. Interestingly, Hochschild does not comment on the needs of the single mother who both works and cares for her family. What are the jobs in the "service sector"? Hochschild doesn't say, but he is probably referring to openings for nurses and medical technicians. In addition, the eighties saw an enormous increase in the number of women who became lawyers, doctors, and business administrators. And if inflation has been lower in the last decade, higher prices for real estate and other worldly goods, higher taxes, and more inflated expectations for standards of living have created the increased need for a second income. What interests us most about Hochschild's opening sentence is its imagery: households that "bear the footprints" of exterior trends live with something foreign and vaguely threatening. Ask your students how they respond to the metaphor as well as to the literal meaning of the sentence. We are also interested in Hochschild's use of the phrase "stalled revolution" at the end of his second paragraph. "Revolution" suggests a massive change bound to occur, and "stalled" suggests a measure of hope: the revolution has not yet come, but it will come. How do your students imagine the revolution? And do they look forward to it, or, in their opinion, has it already occurred?

Ask your class if they believe that men should share equally in caring for children and doing housework. The discussion will, very likely, anticipate answers to our fourth question, about the failure of men to adapt to women's working. Most men are equable about women going to work, but will the men scrub toilets and take out the garbage?

To answer our sixth question, we don't know why the United States does not have what Hochschild calls a "pro-family policy," but we'll make some guesses. Companies see concessions to the two-income family as reducing their profits; politicians, dependent on financial support from business, do not wish to antagonize business leaders; businesses are still largely controlled by men; politicians are still mostly male; and underneath lie the deep prejudices about women working—"the stalled revolution."

Judy Brady
I Want a Wife (p. 177)

This article first appeared in the premier issue of *Ms.*, so presumably its intended audience is female and its purpose is (as the saying goes) consciousness raising. But readers—male as well as female—can scarcely fail to understand that the essay seeks to be persuasive: it doesn't merely suggest that this is the way things are; rather, it implies that the situation is outrageous and ought to be changed.

Topics for Critical Thinking and Writing

1. Analyze the organization of Brady's essay. (What we have in mind is that she moves from routine duties, to the larger duty of keeping the wife subservient, and finally to the double standard in sex.)

2. Imitating Brady's format and style, write a companion piece from a man's point of view, "I Want a Husband." One kind of imitation, the parody, makes gentle fun of the object imitated by exaggerating the style or obvious content, thus humorously revealing the weaknesses or limitations of the original. You may, then, wish to write not merely an imitation of Brady's essay, but an imitation that mocks it.

3. Compare Brady's essay with Leonard's photograph (text, page 136). Your comparison should include a description of the overt content of each and an analysis of what each implies or assumes about traditional female roles.

Black Elk
High Horse's Courting (p. 180)

Topics for Critical Thinking and Writing

1. Give a writing assignment based on our question 1: an analysis of tone in "High Horse's Courting."

2. Question 2 also lends itself to a writing assignment of 500 to 750 words.

Josh Quittner
Keeping Up with Your Kids (p. 185)

We customarily talk at least briefly about the rhetoric of the assigned readings—Did the title grab you? What strategies does the author use in the opening paragraph?—and we think Quittner's writing comes off pretty well. But chiefly, of course, the essay is valuable because of the issues it raises. Our questions in the text direct readers largely toward argumentative topics, e.g., question 6: "If you had an adolescent child, would you use a filter to prevent the child from visiting certain sites? Why, or why not?" We don't know if there is a right answer, but we are confident that such a question will provoke lively responses. The instructor's job will probably be to remind students that they should support their responses with *reasons*—the "why, or why not" of our question.

Celia E. Rothenberg
Child of Divorce (p. 191)

Students find Rothenberg's essay interesting primarily because of its unusual subject, a happy divorced family. We like to point out, however, that while having an unusual subject helps to create interest, it's only the beginning; the writer must convince readers early on that she has something to say on the subject, that although unusual, the subject will in some ways be familiar, and that the story will be well told. Rothenberg's essay is a good occasion to point out the utility of a thesis sentence. The last sentence of her second paragraph announces her thesis: "It is only recently, however, that I have realized how much patience and understanding went into achieving that sense of belonging and love, and how achieving it was part of the long and often painful process for us of divorce and healing." We are all familiar enough, perhaps too familiar, with the "long and often painful" part of divorce. Our interest is piqued by the promise of coming to understand with the writer how a "sense of belonging and love" emerged from it, how the "healing" was created. There's a problem here, even a mystery, with a solution. The thesis sentence reveals the problem and promises the solution; in short, it creates suspense.

Is Rothenberg's account credible? She establishes credibility early by conceding that one might assume that growing up with divorced parents was "rather dreary" (paragraph 2) and later by labeling her family "exceptional" (paragraph 17). Exceptional or not, they probably shared the same "needs and hopes of all families" she supposes, reasonably enough (in paragraph 16). Credibility is also established by Rothenberg's attention to the specific details in the memories she summons up. Ask students which scenes they remember from her account, and you will probably hear about the checkers-by-mail game, or of the mother turning off lights and closing each window and door in the new house (and life), or of the family at Shabbos, the father still at the head of the table, and the brother's friends from college crowded around it. The final paragraph, though a conclusion that sums up the rest, is also specific. We see the family at dinner contributing their own ideas and styles to a memoir, and then the writer herself, alone, late at night in her dormitory room.

Topic for Critical Thinking and Writing

Our first question in the text, "What are your earliest memories of your family?" lends itself well to a writing assignment, in an essay, a journal entry, or both.

Jamaica Kincaid
Girl (p. 196)

Jamaica Kincaid, like her fictional heroines, lived in Antigua, a much-doted-on only child, until she was seventeen, when she came to the United States to continue her education. In an interview in the *New York Times Book Review* (April 7, 1985, p. 6) she says, "I did sort of go to college but it was such a dismal failure. I just educated myself, if that's possible."

In "Girl" we meet an unnamed girl in her early adolescence, under the constant tutelage of her mother for her coming role as a woman. The mother is a powerful presence, shrewd and spirited as well as overprotective and anxious about her daughter's burgeoning sexuality. The girl is attentive to her mother and mostly submissive; we sense that it is through her reverie that we hear her mother's monologue, which the daughter interrupts briefly, only twice. But the repetition of instruction and correction in the monologue, especially of the incessant "this is how to," suggests the tension between the two that we know, from our own experience, will lead to a confrontation that will permanently alter the relationship. Despite the references to the island culture, which provide the story's rich, exotic texture, the central drama of coming-of-age could be happening anywhere.

Robert Hayden
Those Winter Sundays (p. 198)

Students can learn something about writing by thinking about the length of the six sentences that constitute this poem. The first stanza consists of a fairly long sentence (four and a half lines) and a short one (half a line, completing the fifth line of the poem). The brevity of that second sentence reinforces the content—that no one thought about the father—and the brevity also, of course, adds emphasis by virtue of its contrast with the leisurely material that precedes it. Similarly, the sixth sentence, much shorter than the fifth, adds emphasis, an emphasis made more emphatic by the repetition of "What did I know?"

Next a confession: we thought about glossing "offices" in the last line, for students will almost surely misinterpret the word, thinking that it refers to places where white-collar workers do their tasks. But we couldn't come up with a concise gloss that would convey the sense of ceremonious and loving performance of benefits. And it may be just as well to spend some class time on this important word because the thing as well as the word may be unfamiliar to many students. After the word has been discussed, the poem may be read as a splendid illustration of an "office." Like the father in the poem, who drives out the cold and brings warmth (by means of love, of course, as well as coal) to an unknowing child, an "austere and lonely" writer performs an office, shaping experience for another person's use.

One may want to raise the question in class of whether the knowledge that the author was black affects the poem's meaning.

The most important books for the study of Hayden are *Collected Poems*, ed. Frederick Glaysher (1985), and *Collected Prose*, foreword by William Meredith, ed. Frederick Glaysher (1984). Students can begin with this cogent introduction: Fred M. Fetrow, *Robert Hayden* (1984). And, for more depth and detail, they can next consult John Hatcher, *From the Auroral Darkness: The Life and Poetry of Robert Hayden* (1984).

A Casebook on Gay Marriage

The "M" Word and Religion

Most desk dictionaries, in their first definition of *marriage*, use pretty much the same words: *marriage* is "a legal union of a man and woman as husband and wife." We were not surprised to find "a man and woman," but we were surprised to find "a legal union" rather than "a sacred union" or "a ritual administered by a representative of a church," or some such thing. Which gets us to our point: for most people (so it seems to us) *marriage* is associated with religion, and we hear a good deal about "the sanctity of marriage," but in fact marriage is largely a civil ceremony. In the Commonwealth of Massachusetts, where the writer of this page lives, the clergy who solemnize most marriages can do so because the Commonwealth has *legally* invested them with the right to perform marriages. Thus, a rabbi, priest, or minister says (or should say), "By the authority invested in me by the Commonwealth of Massachusetts, I pronounce you husband and wife." Again, the cleric's authority to perform marriages comes from the Commonwealth.

In the earliest days of Christianity, the Christian church of course had no such authority; not until 325 A.D., when Christianity became the official religion of the Roman empire, did the church play a significant role in marriage. From the ninth century onward we hear of couples going to the church door to get the blessing of the priest, and even though the Roman Catholic Church did not for centuries require a priest to be present at a wedding ceremony, it is probably fair to say that in the Western world for the last thousand years the church has dominated the institution of marriage. (Having said this, we must mention that in the early history of the United States, because clergymen were few and the population was scattered, common-law marriages were widely recognized as legal. If you lived with someone and you said you were married, the law recognized you as married. This condition is still true in several states.) Although the church's dominance has been greatly eroded in the last hundred years, many people—including persons who rarely attend church—wish to have their marriage in a church or synagogue.

In short, most people (so we gather) do not want a marriage that might seem to be merely a civil union; they want a marriage that is sanctified by a religious authority. And this sort of union—a marriage rather than a "civil union"—apparently is what some gay people also want. Why? A civil union in some states will bring a gay partner certain legal and financial privileges, for instance, health benefits, the privilege of visiting (as "family" or "next of kin") a partner who is hospitalized, bereavement leave, authority over funeral arrangements, etc. Why isn't this enough for gay people? Because they see that the world around them regards marriage as something better, something higher—what one writer (we can't recall the source) called the gold standard of human relationships. Most gay couples were brought up in straight families, where marriage is usually seen as something very special, not just a legal relationship, and the gays want to be part of this special thing, this relationship that almost everyone says is much more than a "civil union." These gay people want the wedding cake, the tearful mothers, the white limousine, the blessings of the clergy, and the social status that is conveyed when the state recognizes a romantic relationship. And they want these things now.

But can Jewish and Christian clergy confer their blessing? We don't have to tell you that there is much dispute. Hebrew scripture clearly disapproves of homosexual activity: Leviticus 20.13 says, "If a man also lie with mankind, as he lieth with a woman, both of them have committed an abomination: they shall surely be put to death." But Hebrew scripture also prescribes stoning to death for premarital sex and for adultery (Deuteronomy 22.15–24), and we don't hear anyone citing this text as a guide for contemporary behavior. Further, the brother of a man who dies without leaving a son is obliged to marry the widow (Deuteronomy 25.5–10). Most rabbis today depart from the scripture here and elsewhere. To the best of our knowledge, Jesus said nothing about homosexuality, and Paul made only a few fleeting references to it. And while we are talking about the Judeo-Christian tradition, we should mention that the Hebrew patriarchs practiced polygamy (Genesis 29.15–30) and took concubines (Genesis 16.1–2), so it is simply untrue to say that the Bible recognizes only the union of one man with one woman. (For comments on polygamy among the ancient Hebrews, see Michael L. Satlow, *Jewish Marriage in Antiquity* [2001]. The book is not easy reading, but as we see it, Satlow argues that Jewish society was fundamentally polygamous, and the chief purposes of marriage were procreation and the establishment of male social identity, i.e., a male became a man by becoming a patriarch, an authoritarian figure who dominated a family.)

In any case, why are we talking about the Hebrew Bible and the New Testament, since the establishment clause of the First Amendment says Americans should *not* let religious views determine the laws of the nation? We are talking about the Bible because the fact is, most of the legislators in our history have been Christians or Jews, and their thinking has left a mark on our laws. Thus, the *New York Times* (August 21, 2004, p. A 15) quotes Representative Mark Souder, a conservative Republican from Indiana: "To ask me to check my Christian beliefs at the public door is to ask me to expel the Holy Spirit from my life when I serve as a congressman, and that I will not do." We hasten to add that this is not a matter of Republicans versus Democrats, the right versus the left; when Senator Joseph Lieberman was campaigning for vice president in 2000, as Al Gore's running mate, he often said that his values were rooted in the Bible. Indeed, the fact that moral passion based on religious faith underlies much liberal thought was especially evident in the civil rights movement. Further, whether or not they attend church regularly, most Americans believe in God, and politicians know this; it is almost impossible to hear a speech of a candidate for the presidency that does not end with "God bless you all, and God bless America," or some such sentiment.

Still, religious attitudes toward marriage have changed, at least in some respects. For most of the history of our country, it would have been impossible for a divorced man to be elected president, yet in 1980 Ronald Reagan, divorced, was elected to the presidency with the strong support of Evangelical Christians. And the attitudes of the states and of the federal government have also changed. Until late in the twentieth century about one-third of the states prohibited interracial marriage; in 1967 the U.S. Supreme Court struck down these laws, arguing (in the words of Chief Justice Warren) that "the freedom to marry has long been recognized as one of the vital personal rights essential to the orderly pursuit of happiness by free men." (Today we would add "and by free women.") In 1987 the Supreme Court regarded marriage as so fundamental that it could not be denied to prison inmates, some of whose other constitutional rights are regularly abrogated. The issue of the role of the states, as opposed to the federal government, is touched on in the *New York Times* editorial that we reprint in the text.

Bibliographic note: Because the issue is so current, the daily newspaper probably is the best source, but if you want to read a book or two about the changing nature of marriage in the United States, we recommend E. J. Graff, *What Is Marriage For?* (1999, slightly revised 2004), and Nancy Cott, *Public Vows: A History of Marriage and the Nation* (2000). See also, for a balanced account of the issue, Evan Gerstmann, *Same-Sex Marriage and the Constitution* (2004). For two books arguing on behalf of gay marriage, see Evan Wolfson, *Why Marriage Matters: America, Equality, and Gay People's Right to Marry* (2004), and George Chauncey, *Why Marriage? The History Shaping Today's Debate Over Gay Equality* (2004).

Summary of Pro and Con Arguments
Concerning Gay Marriage

So far as we can tell from our reading, the chief arguments concerning gay marriage are these:

Pro

1. If marriage is limited to persons of the opposite sex, human rights are violated. The Human Rights Act of 1977 says, "Every individual shall have an equal opportunity . . . to participate in all aspects of life." The Constitution guarantees each person's right to "life, liberty, and the pursuit of happiness," and it seems to be widely agreed that in pursing happiness one ought to be allowed to marry the person whom one loves. It also seems to be widely agreed that married people are happier than single ones—at least we have read about a couple of polls that came to this conclusion. (May we here interject a moment of levity? A cartoon in *The New Yorker*, March 1, 2004, p. 8, shows a middle-aged man and woman in their living room. The man, holding a newspaper from which he presumably has been reading, says to his wife, "Gays and lesbians getting married— haven't they suffered enough?")
2. Marriage confers numerous material benefits (pensions, health coverage, property rights, citizenship).
3. "Civil unions" or "domestic partnerships" are not the equivalent of marriage; these terms stigmatize the relationship as something less than a loving relationship.
4. The fact that the Bible condemns homosexual relations is irrelevant. And if the views of the Bible were relevant, we would practice polygamy and would regard wives as the property of their husbands.
5. Gay marriage promotes fidelity and family life. Gay couples who adopt children have an added incentive to stay together. Further, there is no convincing evidence that children brought up by gay couples are less stable than children brought up by heterosexuals.
6. The old view was that marriage transformed a male into a husband, a female into a wife—which is to say that it established the man as the ruler of a family; the man gained power, the woman lost power. In the last hundred or so years we have seen marriage change into an institution whereby relations approach equality. Gay marriage is in harmony with this view of marriage; much of the opposition to gay marriage is rooted in an outmoded patriarchal (oppressive) view of the idea of marriage.
7. The mere fact that some people are so strongly opposed to the idea of gay marriage is evidence that marriage is esteemed more highly than "civil union," i.e., marriage is a special condition of superior value, and this condition is being withheld from certain people.

Con

1. Homosexuality is unnatural, illegal, and condemned by the Bible.
2. A homosexual union cannot produce children, and a marriage that lacks children is especially vulnerable.
3. If there are children, whether from a previous marriage or adopted, the children are at a disadvantage; children need a father and a mother.
4. The very idea of gay marriage degrades—debases, devalues—heterosexual marriage.
5. If two persons of the same sex are allowed to marry, we are on a slippery slope. Next will come polygamy and polyandry, incest, and bestiality.

Where We Are Today (i.e., at the time of this writing, autumn, 2004)

Several cities have given legal recognition to domestic partnership. For instance, Berkeley, California has extended health benefits to the unmarried partners of city workers. But same-sex *marriage* was not the issue; in fact, this legal recognition covered heterosexual partnerships as well as homosexual ones. Probably the most significant turn of events occurred in February 2004, when the Supreme Judicial Court of Massachusetts ruled that marriage—including same-sex marriage—is a constitutional right. This decision is far more significant than the decision of Mayor Gavin Newsom of San Francisco, who also in February 2004 authorized the city to issue licenses to same-sex couples. Mayor Newsom argued that the state law that limited marriage to the union of one man and one woman was unconstitutional, but the California Supreme Court ruled in August 2004 that the mayor did not have the right to authorize City Hall to issue the licenses, and the court therefore declared the several thousand San Francisco marriages "void and of no legal effect from their inception." The important point is this: the California court did *not* address the issue of the constitutionality of a state law limiting marriage to a union of one man and one woman. It simply said that the mayor did not have the authority to order the issuing of licenses to same-sex couples. In short, the Massachusetts court decision, legitimizing homosexual unions, is what has provoked the talk of a constitutional amendment banning same-sex marriage.

Ellen Willis
Can Marriage Be Saved? (p. 199)

As we understand this essay, the question is not "Can Marriage Be Saved?" but "Should Marriage Be Saved?" and Willis's answer is No, or, rather, OK, save it for those who want "a social ritual reflecting religious or personal conviction," but it should have no legal meaning. Given this view, she sees the push for gay marriage as both subversive and conservative. It is subversive in that it undermines the patriarchal view of marriage, i.e., the view that a father rules over a dependent wife and children (paragraph 4), but it is conservative in that it reinforces the prevailing system in which married people are given benefits denied to unmarried people. As Willis sees it, gay activists who are fighting for gay marriage are really saying, in effect, that they want to enter the privileged circle—they want a piece of the action—and they are not at all bothered by the inequity of a system that privileges marriage.

One of the commonest arguments against legalizing gay marriage is that it opens the door to plural marriages (polygamy, polyandry) and even to bestiality. Willis in her fifth paragraph seems untroubled by what she calls "group marriage." (She does not address the possiblity of a marriage between a man or woman and a dog, but opponents of gay marriage commonly introduce such a relation and see gay marriage as the first step down a slippery slope.) What response, if any, can be made to Willis's position?

Andrew Sullivan
Here Comes the Groom:
A (Conservative) Case for Gay Marriage (p. 201)

Sullivan's essay is lucid; the difficulties that it may cause in class are not from any obscurity in the essay but from the boldness of the thesis and the depth of feelings that students may hold on the issue.

Twenty years ago this essay was inconceivable, and even ten years ago teachers might have felt that they could not teach such an essay, partly because no one would dare to express support for any ideas in it, but homosexuality and lesbianism are now out of the closet (even if every gay and lesbian is not). Most colleges and universities have some sort of gay/lesbian association that does not hesitate to keep the matter in the public eye. But of course one need not be a gay or a lesbian to support part or all of Sullivan's argument; some straight students may defend it, and, for that matter, some gay/lesbian students may attack it on the grounds that it seeks to assimilate them into the bourgeois straight world.

This last point perhaps needs a bit of clarification. Twenty years ago homosexuals—if they spoke about homosexuality at all—were likely to say, in effect, "We are just like you, except for what we do in bed." That is, their position was pretty much that of the early members of the women's movement, who said to men, "We are just like you, so we want the jobs and the salaries that you have." Today, however, in a world of identity politics, where some people insist that they are distinctive by virtue of their color, or ethnicity, or gender—many feminists today say that women have distinctive ways of thinking—some gays and lesbians similarly insist that their sexual preference makes them essentially different from others. In this view, everything about them differs from straight people. The counterpart to the new feminism is "queer theory," which turns the old plea for tolerance (based on the essential sameness of all people) upside down and in effect says to straights, "Except for what we do in bed, we are utterly different from you."

If you think that no one in your class may be willing to defend any aspect of Sullivan's essay, and if your campus has some sort of gay/lesbian group, you may want to ask the group if it wishes to send a member to participate in the discussion.

Lisa Schiffren
Gay Marriage, an Oxymoron (p. 206)

This selection functions nicely in the classroom: it is forthright and concise, and students quickly move to support or challenge Schiffren's position. But for us the main value of "Gay Marriage, an Oxymoron" is the opportunity it provides for the study of "the language of argument"—how this author organizes and accents her language in order to present her claims. What is the difference between stating one's opinion and making an argument?

Consider, for example, the third paragraph. Here, we ask students to comment on the phrase "momentous change." It's not simply a "change" but a "momentous" one (i.e., weighty, crucially important, of significant consequence). Notice the similar deployment of adjectives in the next lines: not just a "redefinition" but a "radical redefinition"; not just an "institution" but a "most fundamental institution"; not just "debate" but "no real debate."

The obvious strength of this kind of writing is that it is forceful: Schiffren is taking a stand, is very decisive about it, and is determined to make an impact on the reader. The weakness or limitation of such writing is that it can feel highly coercive, as though the issue is absolutely clear-cut, with the reader allowed only one acceptable response.

When we focus on Schiffren's essay, then, we ask the students to discuss her choices of language. We'd like them to bear in mind the fine line between stating an opinion and presenting an argument. Can we say that Schiffren is presenting an argument? If she is, where is the evidence and how effectively and convincingly is it offered? If she is not, what is her purpose? What does she intend to accomplish?

"Gay Marriage, an Oxymoron" is also useful for inviting students to think carefully about the context in which a piece of writing appears. The essay was written for the op-ed page of the *New York Times*. What can a writer *do* in the space allotted for an op-ed piece? Is it really possible to make an argument, or does the assignment call for something else? When the reader of a newspaper turns to the op-ed page, what does he or she expect from the pieces printed there? What are the elements of a good op-ed essay?

One of the key lessons about paper-writing we try to teach students is "Know the nature of the job you've been asked to perform." If you are writing an op-ed piece, such an assignment calls for an approach, a strategy, that differs from that for a scholarly publication or a research seminar. If you are told that your piece for the op-ed page cannot exceed 750 words, then you are obliged to work within this boundary. You cannot *do* in it what you can in an assignment that allows for 1,500 words.

Often, we find that students run into trouble in their paper-writing because they haven't brought to the fore the nature of the assignment and the amount of "space" they have been given for it, and Schiffren's essay is very useful for highlighting these issues. For this essay, as for others, we seek to explore what the writer of the selection is saying, and, equally important (or more), what students can learn from it about how to make their own writing better.

Anonymous
Gay Marriage in the States (p. 208)

We include the editorial chiefly for two reasons: it raises the issue of the role of the states, and it provoked some interesting letters of response.

As to the first point, the role of the states as "social laboratories for the nation," we do and we don't understand the point. Yes, we can understand that the issue is discussed on the state level, and a variety of answers may be proposed. What we don't understand is this: if the U.S. Supreme Court could throw out state laws that prohibited intermarriage among races, who really cares what the state laboratories produce, since the deciding view will be that of the U.S. Supreme Court? (A word about the prohibition against interracial marriage. Those days were not so long ago, at least by the standard of the writer of this page, who has a white friend who in the early 1960s taught in Virginia. This friend then married a Japanese woman and was therefore required to resign his position at a university and to leave the state. The law doubtless was intended to prevent blacks and whites from marrying, but it was extended to include whites and Asians. Again, all this within living memory, not in a remote past.)

A moment ago we said that we do and we don't understand the idea that the states are laboratories, since the U.S. Supreme Court can reject the findings of the state laboratories. But perhaps the apparent inconsistency is reconciled thus: although the Court can indeed declare a state law unconstitutional, it is a pretty conservative institution, and if indeed it ever votes to declare unconstitutional a state's law banning gay marriage, it will not do so until a large number of states have enacted laws approving gay marriage. We say this because the Court was very slow to rule against anti-miscegenation laws. California ruled against them in 1948, and in the next nineteen years, fourteen other states also ruled against them. That is, before the U. S. Supreme Court ruled in 1967, in *Loving v. Virginia*, it was pretty clear that the nation as a whole disapproved of laws prohibiting interracial marriage. In this sense, then, the states are laboratories, working things out, and when a large number of states have come to a similar conclusion on a social issue, apparently the U.S. Supreme Court then takes up the matter and concurs. Most onlookers believe it will be a very long time (maybe never) before a large number of states legalize gay marriage.

Letters of Response by Marcy E. Feller and Bill Banuchi

Letter by Marcy E. Feller: Like Willis, Feller sees marriage as essentially a religious matter, and she suggests that we should consider legislating civil unions for straight as well as gay couples. Compare this letter with Willis's first paragraph, in which she quotes the mayor of San Francisco, who said that such a proposal would enrage married people—though Willis in her second paragraph makes the point that she takes a very different view. We suggest that you ask your students how they feel about making marriage a purely religious matter.

Letter by the Reverend Bill Banuchi: This letter is especially interesting because it introduces an analogy: just as gold would be devalued if the government declared that sandstone will now be called gold, so marriage will be devalued if same-sex couples are allowed to marry. How good is this analogy? First of all, we should remember that *all* analogies are, so to speak, false. The idea of an analogy is this: A is like B in ways 1, 2, and 3, so A is also like B in 4. But of course A is not B; A and B are different things, and they therefore necessarily *differ* in some ways. If in an election year during a war we say "Don't change horses in midstream," we are saying that a war is like a turbulent stream, and that we should stay with our leader until things calm down. But a war (or a depression, or whatever) is *not* a stream, and choosing a new leader is *not* really much like changing horses. In short, though the figure has considerable power, it is scarcely a convincing argument. Ditto for the following analogy: just as the body is strengthened by exercise, so the mind is strengthened by the exercise of (say) learning Latin. (There are good reasons for learning Latin, but surely no one today believes that it "strengthens the mind.") You may want to refer students to our brief discussion of *analogy* in the glossary at the back of the text.

Certainly Banuchi is correct in saying that if tomorrow the government declares that sandstone is valued equally with gold, the decree devalues the gold we have. An ounce of gold will in fact become virtually worthless. But how does calling a gay union "marriage" devalue the straight marriage of John and Jane Doe? Will their love for each other somehow decrease? Will their friends and children hold them in less esteem? Will they lose certain financial benefits? Will their jobs be in jeopardy? Banuchi says that marriage is "an unalienable right ordained by nature, and nature's God." Not everyone will agree with him, but even if one does agree, in what way does the legalizing of gay marriage "devalue" the marriage of someone who holds this view? Such a person will still feel that his or her marriage is "ordained by nature, and nature's God," and will probably feel that gay marriage is not in fact marriage at all. But is the straight marriage "devalued"? Or, to get back to our question, does the analogy make sense?

7

IDENTITIES

Illustrations

Dorothea Lange
Grandfather and Grandchildren Awaiting Evacuation Bus, Hayward, California, May 9, 1942 (p. 214)

For some background about the evacuation or relocation of Japanese and Japanese Americans from the states on the Pacific Coast, see our discussion of Yamada's "To the Lady," in this manual, p. 165.

Lange, working for the War Relocation Authority, photographed the proceedings as part of a program documenting the relocation. What can we say about the picture that we reproduce? Lange probably asked the family to pose, and she may have created the composition (the grandfather seated, the smaller boy in front of the taller boy), but she didn't create the tags, she didn't create the little packages wrapped in newspaper, and she didn't create the expressions on the faces. Most interesting is the grandfather's grim and dignified manner, chiefly created by his face but also by his erect posture and his cane. Also interesting is the echo of the grandfather in the smaller boy's expression and the angle of his head.

Marion Post Wolcott
Behind the Bar, Birney, Montana (p. 215)

No one can say that the messages are not clear. And there is something for everyone: a patriotic banner; a pinup girl; a courteous, even plaintive, sign asking for the clientele not to cause embarrassment by requesting credit or loans; a sign restricting the sale of beer. Presumably Indians can buy the packs of cigarettes and matches arranged at the right and the packages of tobacco and potato chips scarcely visible at the left, but beer is out of their reach. The courtesy implied in "Please don't ask" on the relatively light sign about credit and loans is missing from the sign about beer, where an emphatic "positively" reinforces the dark message. Apparently the proprietors find no inconsistency in announcing their proud allegiance to a country that stands for "justice for all" while discriminating against Native Americans. The moral ugliness of the unintended irony (unintended by the proprietors but seized on by the photographer) is almost matched by the visual ugliness of this still life. An earlier still life (say, a Dutch painting) would have shown food, perhaps including a half-cut loaf of bread, and dishes or utensils suggesting civility, especially hospitality. This photograph reveals a different way of life.

Short Views

Topics for Critical Thinking and Writing

1. What examples support Mead's analysis? Can you think of any counter-examples?

2. What does Beauvoir mean by "This has always been a man's world"? If it is true, how can one explain it?

3. What is Zangwill's vision of the future of racial identity in America? What has been left out of his crucible?

4. Martin Luther King Jr.'s sentence has been widely remembered and quoted since he spoke it. What makes it so memorable? (Analyze the form of the sentence, as well as the content.)

Stephen J. Gould
Women's Brains (p. 218)

Stephen Jay Gould teaches geology, biology, and the history of science at Harvard; his lectures are enormously popular. His monthly columns in *Natural History* magazine also attract a wide readership and have been collected in several best-selling books. "Women's Brains" appears in *The Panda's Thumb: More Reflections on Natural History,* a collection centered on evolutionary theory.

What makes his writing, often on arcane topics, so attractive? For one thing, he does not condescend to the reader. Words of moderate difficulty, such as "misogynist," "chimera," "denigrated," "juxtaposition," and "enigma," crop up with a frequency that might disconcert some freshmen. But he doesn't go out of his way to be difficult either, and when he uses a word likely to be unfamiliar to nonspecialists, like "anthropometry" or "craniometry," in the second paragraph, he immediately defines it.

He assumes that a reader enjoys a little mental exercise, but he doesn't make excessive demands. His essays are brief, relaxed, and pungent. He chooses a cogent example of a point he is making, explains it, and stops. He doesn't overqualify an argument or overexplain a point. Now and then he underexplains. In "Women's Brains," for example, Maria Montessori makes an abrupt appearance (in paragraph 15) and it isn't until the fourth sentence of the paragraph that we see her connection to Broca's research or to Gould's argument. And the passages from *Middlemarch* with which Gould begins and ends his essay are not, in our opinion, as illuminating as Gould seems to think they are. But we're not thrown off by these eccentricities. We'd characterize Gould's style as quirky but not boring.

Another feature of his style that we find attractive but that some students might find puzzling is his frequent recourse to irony. Since some students tend to read everything that appears in a textbook as if it were nothing more (or less) than the literal truth, we pause briefly over a few instances of irony. For example, in the second paragraph Gould tells us that "Anthropometry, or measurement of the human body . . . remained popular until intelligence testing replaced skull measurement as a favored device for making invidious comparisons among races, classes, and sexes." When, also in paragraph 2, he says that the work of Broca's disciples "won high esteem as a jewel of nineteenth-century science," students might need some help in seeing that the slightly elevated language is ironic; it reveals Gould's distance from that "high esteem." Similarly, when Gould calls Gustave Le Bon "chief misogynist of Broca's school," he is not bestowing an honorific.

But the chief attraction of Gould's writing for the nonscientist is his pleasure in illuminating the cultural context of scientific ideas.

Topic for Critical Thinking and Writing

What is your understanding, from reading Gould's essay, of "biological labeling"? If you have had any first-hand experience of biological labeling, explain the experience and your reaction to it.

Katha Pollitt
Why Boys Don't Play with Dolls (p. 223)

Pollitt's first sentence, with its assertion that although NOW was founded 28 years ago, "boys still like trucks and girls still like dolls," might cause a reader to suspect that she will argue that biology determines behavior—that *nature* triumphs over *nurture*. Her third sentence, which can be taken as a rhetorical question, seems to further this point, but even a rhetorical question at least theoretically can be answered in more than one way. (An interesting thing about rhetorical questions is that they embody an assumption; the questioner assumes that the hearer shares the assumption, but of course this assumption itself may be false.) Pollitt asks a question, and readers may think they know what answer she expects, but at this stage they can't be certain. And she will go on, engagingly, to surprise her readers.

The answer she gives is that despite our claims that we discourage stereotypical behavior, we often encourage it or at least tolerate it, as when a mother allows her daughter to give a Barbie doll as a gift to a friend. In paragraph 9 Pollitt speaks especially strongly: How many moms will be happy if their sons prefer to spend the weekend writing in a diary or baking, rather than engaging in sports?

Speaking of "moms," we think it is worth calling students' attention to Pollitt's abundant use of colloquial words, for instance, "kids" rather than "children" in the final paragraph. In our experience, students are afraid to use colloquial expressions, and when they do use them they tend to enclose the expressions within quotation marks, thereby calling undue attention to them. It's probably a good thing to warn students against using colloquialisms, especially in academic writing, but it's probably also a good thing to tell them that highly skilled writers can and do use them successfully, even in academic writing. The trick—and it may take years to learn—is to develop an ear, a sense of style, a confidence in one's ability to know how the imagined reader will respond. Our own practice is to discuss the issue—easy to do with Pollitt's essay—cautioning students that when in doubt, the best course is to play it safe and not use colloquialisms but making it clear that such words do have a place in the arsenal of skilled writers.

Paul Theroux
The Male Myth (p. 226)

Theroux's essay offers a definition through reflecting on personal experience. And in the course of defining masculinity, Theroux also defines femininity.

It's worth noting that for all of Theroux's attack on masculine or manly competitiveness and aggression, his own writing is pretty aggressive. A small example: "There is no book hater like a Little League coach." No chance is permitted for the Little League coach to suggest that we look into the matter, or even for the reader to think that this assertion is patently unfair. It's amusing, though, and it does its dirty work very effectively. Immediately after making this assertion, Theroux comes up with the astounding statement that "at their best the arts are pursued by uncompetitive . . . people." (We here omit his assertion, which seems true to us, that these people are "essentially solitary.") Of course Theroux's "at their best" gives him a loophole, but when one thinks of the careers of, say, Milton, Pope, Dostoyevski, Tolstoy, Pound, or Frost—to name only a few of the great literary artists—it's hard to swallow Theroux's assertion that even "at their best" the arts are uncompetitive.

Bharati Mukherjee
Two Ways to Belong in America (p. 230)

First, the title. Although one always suspects that the title of an op-ed piece may be the choice of the editor rather than of the author, still, as readers we must assume the author is responsible for the title. This title, "Two Ways to Belong to America," is pretty bland, but it does announce the topic, and implicitly the thesis too, since it implies that whether one "belongs" in one way or another, one nevertheless belongs.

We imagine that most native-born Americans, and also most naturalized Americans, will be impatient with Bharati Mukherjee's sister, Mira. After all, they may argue, if she likes living here and likes earning a living here, why doesn't she become a citizen? But obviously Mira sees things differently. Judging from this essay, Mira thinks the United States should be grateful to her for her work here. In paragraph 8 Mukherjee tells us that Mira feels "used" and "manipulated." As she sees it, she has invested her "creativity and professional skills into the improvement" of the United States, and she cannot understand why this is not enough. "This is such an unfair way to treat a person who was invited to stay and work here because of her talent," Mira tells Bharati.

It is probably easy for most native-born citizens to feel that someone who comes here and makes a living here ought to become a citizen. That's why in our third question we ask readers, if they found themselves working abroad for much of a lifetime, would they become citizens of the country in which they were residing? It's our guess that they would not. An American who spent 25 years teaching school in Korea, or working as a translator and newspaper correspondent in Japan, or serving as a professor of American literature in Germany, might well feel that he or she had made significant contributions to the country and yet was by no means obliged to become a citizen. Why, then, do many of us believe that a foreigner who comes to the United States, and remains for a lifetime, ought to become a citizen? Put bluntly, we may think thus: If they don't like us well enough to become one of us, why don't they get out? Presumably we feel that what America offers this person is greater than what the person gives to America, and the person ought to recognize the benefit that America confers by, so to speak, embracing it fully.

Again, our third question seeks to help students to see things from a different point of view. On the other hand, Mira to us sounds unpleasantly self-satisfied. When she says, "I've invested my creativity and professional skills into the improvement of *this* country's pre-school system," one is tempted to retort, "Oh, yes, we would have suffered greatly without you. And by the way, if you are so attached to India, how come you didn't bestow your creativity and your professional skills on your native land? Are we to believe that your presence here is a sort of Mother Teresa–like act of charity because our need for creative teachers is greater than India's need?"

We are saying that we think Bharati Mukherjee has called attention to an extremely interesting issue, but it is our guess that students, including those who do not intend to become American citizens, will find it a bit difficult to argue on behalf of Mira's position.

Emily Tsao
Thoughts of an Oriental Girl (p. 233)

Tsao's essay is, in our opinion, successful both as an argument (against "political correctness") and as an exposition (of pressures to modify values, experienced by many entering college students). Students can, as they say, both "relate" to it and emulate it as well. To examine the argument, we look first at the title, with the first instance of irony in the essay. Other instances can be found in the first paragraph (there is, of course, no "politically correct dictionary") and in paragraphs 10, 13, and 14. We find it useful to ask students to examine irony because, although their speech abounds in irony, freshmen (first-year students!) often don't see it in what they read unless they're asked to. And we encourage them to use irony (though not sarcasm) in writing, particularly in writing arguments. (We commonly bring to class samples of verbal irony, including sarcasm, for discussion. What works? What doesn't?)

We also call attention to Tsao's use of details to make her point. (The words "Be specific" litter the margins of papers we return.) As one example, we examine paragraph 6: "Men don't drink themselves sick at keg parties every weekend, ask Dad for money, or take laundry home to Mom."

We suspect that within a year or so of writing this essay Tsao was using the words "women" and "men" to replace "girls" and "boys" or "guys." But we also suspect that her irritation about being called a person of color did not diminish but increase. In paragraph 13 she writes, "Minority groups want new labels to give themselves a more positive image, but unless the stereotypes disappear as well, is it really going to help very much?" This is a good question to pose to the class, to be answered, perhaps, in an essay. Another essay assignment: If you have suffered from others' use of stereotypes, explain what the stereotypes were, how they were communicated, and what your reaction was, or what you wish it had been.

Gloria Naylor
A Question of Language (p. 235)

Naylor asserts that written language is inferior to spoken language, and her discussion of the words "nigger" and "girl" in the body of her essay appear to confirm her point. In her childhood, she understood that the word "nigger," spoken in her family circle and with the appropriate inflection, referred to a male with admiration, whereas the plural "niggers" expressed contempt. But when the word "nigger" was spat out at her by a schoolmate (presumably white), she did not know what the word meant, except that it was bad. There is nothing here to disbelieve, and most of us (most members of the class) can offer memories of similar experiences with words and ethnic epithets, spoken within our particular group or from without.

But of course it is Naylor's skill with the written word that recreates from her specific memories of spoken words those inflections and contexts for us, which include us, along with readers of *The New York Times*, in her community. And we're struck by the way her essay, from time to time, captures the tone of conversation, not the conversation she remembers (although she does that superbly too) but the one with us. When in the second paragraph she says, "I'm not going to enter the debate here about whether it is language that shapes reality or vice versa," or "I will simply take the position that . . . ," or, in the fourteenth paragraph, "I don't agree with the argument that . . . ," the topics may be abstract but the voice is personal; the rhythm is that of a lively conversation.

Jeanne Wakatsuki Houston
Double Identity (p. 238)

The "double identity" of the title is Jeanne Wakatsuki's attempt to be Japanese around Japanese men and to be *hakujin* (Caucasian) around Caucasian men. Her identity is altered further when she marries a Caucasian man; should she put his socks and underwear out for him, as her mother had for her father? The memoir is a pleasant one, and so we find her doing this sometimes, when she felt Japanese, and otherwise not. There are, of course, more serious issues: the problem of cooperation, for example, as a Japanese woman, and competitiveness, which she observes in her husband.

A good way to ask students to read and write about "Double Identity" is to ask each of them to choose a passage and then to imitate it. One might, for example, write, "I have come to accept the cultural hybridness of my personality, to recognize it as a strength and not weakness" and then analyze it in one's own terms. Or, "My world is radically different from my mother's world, and all indications point to an even wider difference in our world from our children's." (One can write about this sentence whether or not one has children. But it might be interesting to imagine children if one has none.)

Richard Rodriguez
A View from the Melting Pot (p. 245)

On one level, this selection is a hard one for us to teach. Bilingual education, affirmative action, etc.: these are issues that we have engaged often in Composition and Rhetoric courses, and we admit that on some days it's something of a challenge to come to them as if they were fresh and dynamic.

The same holds true perhaps for many students. In high school courses or on the debate team, or in other courses in college, it's likely that they have read and written about these issues and discussed them back and forth in the classroom.

But there are advantages for students to working with a familiar set of issues. Because students have some knowledge of the arguments, they may speak with more confidence than they do when the issue is a new one for them. They may speak with more passion in their voices too, because they feel that in this instance, they know what they think.

There are advantages to you as well. You can say to students, "Well, that's an argument we hear frequently, but is it really a good argument?" Or: "Fine, you make a good argument, but isn't there an assumption behind it that you need to be aware of?" You can do some role-playing too. You might say to a student, "I really like the way you make your point; you really make the case well. But how about this: imagine you are on the other side of the issue. How would you answer the argument that you've made so well?"

Oddly enough, then, this Rodriguez selection usually turns out to be very effective as a teaching tool. The truth is that our students are not very good at making arguments—as opposed to stating their positions. Nor are they as adept as they should be at critical thinking. With a piece like this one, you can keep bringing to the fore the elements of an *effective argument*, and, related to it, the type of critical thinking that the making of an effective argument requires.

One quick tip for a writing assignment, which we have given, and with good results:

State your position on this issue in a single crisp, clear sentence. Then, give your best argument for it in a paragraph of five or so sentences. Now take a breath, and make the best argument you can *against* the argument you just made. Good. Now that you have done that, say which of these arguments is better and explain why.

David Brooks
People Like Us (p. 251)

Brooks uses examples throughout his essay, beginning with his first paragraph. After eliciting class response to our first topic ("Indicate two or three passages in which you find [concrete examples]") we are likely to analyze the first paragraph. The power of examples comes, first of all, from their liveliness—they attract our attention—and, second, they lead to our understanding of and probably to our assent to Brooks's point: "We don't really care about diversity all that much in America, even though we talk about it a great deal."

In addition to his use of examples, Brooks also offers appeals to authority—the marketing firm Claritas in paragraph 8, *The Bell Curve* in paragraph 11, the Center for the Study of Popular Culture and the American Enterprise Institute in paragraph 13. And, although Brooks wears it lightly, his essay is based on research. Look, for example, at his reference to the 2000 census in paragraph 5.

We also cite Brooks's style as support for his argument. In addition to observing the persuasiveness of Brooks's examples, we also want our students to observe the effect of his alternating long sentences with short sentences (again, the first paragraph offers a useful example) and Brooks's clear focus on his audience. He uses the first person easily, and right from the start aligns himself with his reader: "We don't really care about diversity . . . in America. . . ." In his last paragraphs he addresses his readers directly: ". . . maybe you should take out a subscription to *The Door*, the evangelical humor magazine" and, finally, "Look around at your daily life. Are you really in touch with the broad diversity of American life? Do you care?"

Brent Staples
The "Scientific" War on the Poor (p. 256)

In Brent Staples's title, the word "Scientific" is in quotation marks. The first I.Q. test, designed by Binet, had one purpose: to help segregate learning-disabled children for special schools. The I.Q. tests work no better now, despite the "worship" we give them. "Most scientists concede that they don't really know what 'intelligence' is" (paragraph 3).

Staples gives several examples of his contempt for I.Q. tests; one might go through the article to demonstrate how the writer's purpose and audience dictate his tone. One could begin with the first paragraph. The opening, "Everyone knows the stereotype of the fair-haired executive who owes his office with the view and the six-figure salary to an accident of birth." Who is his audience here? How do we know? Or there is "Daniel Patrick Moynihan's ludicrous claim" that births to single mothers create "a new species." Or "Goddard and his colleagues" who "believed that Nordic peoples were civilization's best" and whose tests demonstrated that "80 percent of all Jews, Italians and Hungarians and nearly 90 percent of Russians were 'feebleminded.'" And so on. In the last paragraph Staples brings up *The Bell Curve*, the motive for his argument, to show that Charles Murray and Richard Hernstein repeat the claim that "I.Q. is mainly inherited." There is no "plausible data" to assert this but only "brutal preconceptions about poverty" and "a basic confusion between pseudoscience and the real thing."

It is not "science" that Murray and Hernstein offer in *The Bell Curve* but history—a history of preconceptions about poor people. Binet had "warned that a 'brutal pessimism' would follow if his test was ever mistaken as a measure of a fixed, unchangeable intelligence." We have not read *The Bell Curve* and we don't know if there is a reasonable difference between Murray and Hernstein's case and Goddard's, for example. The essay is not, however, trying to argue a point, but rather to make things clear to those who, having read about *The Bell Curve*, are anxious about the results. Staples tells us, with some anger, that we have heard all this before and that it is nonsense.

Amy Tan
Snapshot: Lost Lives of Women (p. 258)

We might begin discussion of this piece by asking: In what ways are the lives of the women in the snapshot "lost"?

Tan's first paragraph suggests that they were all but lost from memory. Born in the United States, Tan, as a child looking at the snapshot, saw no connection between these "exotic" women and herself, although the snapshot included three generations of her family. They are lost, in a second way, because her mother, who is in the picture herself, intended to keep their lives secret (paragraph 5) and is ashamed of her own life. Her secret is that her mother was a concubine, and her family consequently had "no position in life." That her mother was raped and forced into concubinage is part of the shame. "We had no face! We belonged to nobody!" (paragraph 13). This is the third way they were "lost."

What does it mean to "belong to nobody"? Another way to begin the class is by reading paragraph 13 and asking this question: To whom could one belong? Do we not "belong" to ourselves? Are we not, as adults at least, legally and morally responsible for our own lives? The tragedies of the women in the snapshot answer this question. Like land, or furniture, or other possessions, they belonged to their husbands. Their position derived from and their fate depended upon the fortunes, status, temperaments, and whims of the men to whom they were married. Since they were owned by their husbands, who might also own second wives and concubines, the women could be and frequently were mistreated and abused. (Two of the women in the snapshot escaped their fates through suicide.) And before they were married, they belonged to their fathers, who saw to it that their wives prepared their daughters for the marriage market by training them to be beautiful.

For a woman to be beautiful in China at the time the snapshot was taken (around 1922) meant that she had small feet, which were provided not by nature (which might or might not have endowed a young girl with a pretty face) but by footbinding. (We call attention to "Look at their bound feet!" in paragraph 1.) This cruel practice (which we have learned about by reading John Fairbank's *Chinabound* [1982], pp. 54–55), began in China at court in the tenth century, spread widely, even among the peasants, and lasted well into the twentieth century. When a girl was between five and seven years old, her feet were wrapped in long, narrow cloths so that the big toe curled back toward the heel and the small toes curled under. In the process, the arch was broken, producing a crevice between the heel and big toe, and the foot became both smaller and narrower. It was, of course, painful and disabling. "Foot-binding," Fairbank writes, "was obviously a hyper-civilized triumph of man over woman. . . . The females fixed themselves, mother teaching daughter, so that they were weaker than men, unable to run away (a man could catch them at a walk), and resigned to being housebound" (p. 55). It is also apparent, Fairbank explains, that "the three inch golden lily was a fetish." Bound feet provided men with "two extra private parts for men to toy with. . . . Thus a sexual fetish, self-perpetuating, reinforced male domination" (p. 55).

Bound feet, evident in the snapshot, are, perhaps, the most exotic fact and symbol of the subjection of women in pre-Communist China. But subjection of women, ownership of them by their husbands, has been part of Western culture too, deriving from Roman law. Although the laws and the status of women have gradually changed since the nineteenth century, the legal subjection of women has left its traces in our culture. Tan's concluding sentence, "These are the women who never let me forget why stories need to be told," defines her purpose in writing this essay and the dominant themes of her fiction.

Pat Mora
Immigrants (p. 262)

At least three voices are heard in Mora's poem: the voice of the immigrant, hoping that his or her child will resemble Americans (WASPs, that is); the voice of the immigrant, fearful that the child will not be liked because the child will not seem sufficiently American; and the ironic voice of the poet, expressing skepticism about the hopes for assimilation to an Anglo-American model.

The almost comic glimpse of imperfect pronunciation given in line 8 ("hallo, babee, hallo")—the speaker of the poem here seems to have a somewhat superior attitude—disappears in the last three lines which, though written in English, sympathetically represent the fear that is thought "in Spanish or Polish." If you discuss these lines, you may want to invite students to express their opinions about why "american" is not capitalized in the last two lines, even though it is capitalized in the first ("the American flag"), and "Spanish" and "Polish" are capitalized. We take it that by not capitalizing "american" in the last two lines the poet implies that it's not all that wonderful to become an "american"; indeed there may be a loss in changing from "Spanish" or "Polish" to "american."

Put it this way: the poem shifts from the eager activity of immigrant parents (presented almost comically in lines 1–7) to a more sympathetic presentation of deep fears in lines 8–14, but the whole is complicated by the author's implied criticism (chiefly through "american") of the immigrants' understandable but mistaken activity.

A Casebook on Race

First, a few provocative quotations that you may want to use in class. They all come from the entry on race in Robert Andrews's *The Columbia Dictionary of Quotations* (1993).

> It's a great shock at the age of five or six to find that in a world of Gary Coopers you are the Indian. (James Baldwin; 1963)

> The new grammar of race is constructed in a way that George Orwell would have appreciated, because its rules make some ideas impossible to express—unless, of course, one wants to be called a racist. (Stephen Carter; 1992)

> In fact, there is clear evidence of black intellectual superiority: in 1984, 92 percent of blacks voted to retire Ronald Reagan, compared to only 36 percent of whites. (Barbara Ehrenreich; 1988)

> I have a dream that my four little children will one day live in a nation where they will not be judged by the color of their skin but by the content of their character. (Martin Luther King Jr.; 1963)

The word *race* first appears in the early sixteenth century, with reference to persons sharing common history; one could speak of "the race of lawyers" as easily as the "race of Britons." It did not acquire a biological meaning until the late eighteenth century, when attention was paid to skin color, hair color, shape of the nose, etc., and these in turn came to be associated with intellectual and moral traits. Thus, in the classification (1735) of Carl von Linné, Europeans have pale skin and are "active, ingenious"; Africans have dark skin and are "lazy . . . and governed by whim"; aboriginal

Americans have reddish skin and are "persevering"; Asians have yellowish skin and are "haughty, miserly." It is important to understand that Linné (and others) allowed for the possibility of evolutionary change. After all, such persons argued, we are all descended from Adam and Eve; we have changed—just look at the racial differences all around us—and it is possible that we will continue to change. Well, perhaps not "we"; perhaps the change will be limited to those others, the non-whites, who will in time evolve and reach white perfection. In the eighteenth century this idea was complemented by Locke's tabula rasa, which emphasized the importance of conditioning.

Perhaps the most (in)famous expression of the idea that whites are superior but that others may in time rise mentally and morally is found in Kipling's "The White Man's Burden," published in 1899, when the United States was victorious in the Spanish-American War. Kipling, the poet of imperialism, invites the United States to accept the burden of improving the minds of its colonial subjects. The first stanza runs thus:

> Take up the White Man's burden—
> Send for the best ye breed—
> Go bind your sons to exile
> To serve your captives' need;
> To wait in heavy harness,
> On fluttered folk and wild—
> Your new caught, sullen peoples,
> Half-devil and half-child.

"Half-devil and half-child" nicely hits the ambiguity of the age: "These darker people seem to be of a different nature from us, almost devils; and yet, they also seem childlike, and maybe with our adult guidance they can be improved, turned into creatures rather like us." But it won't be easy:

> Take up the White Man's burden—
> The savage wars of peace—
> Fill full the mouth of Famine
> And bid the sickness cease;
> And when your goal is nearest
> The end for others sought,
> Watch sloth and heathen Folly
> Bring all your hopes to nought.

Still (we are skipping some stanzas), although white America up to now (1899) has had it easy, and has felt no responsibility to improve the minds of the people whom Kipling in "Recessional" calls "lesser breeds without the Law," with the recent victory over Spain, America has become an imperial power and cannot refuse the responsibilities it acquired through conquest. Gone are the days when Americans could judge themselves only by their own easy standards;

the time has come when they will be judged by the high-minded imperial powers of modern Europe, who know the responsibilities of white power.

> Take up the White Man's burden—
> Have done with childish days—
> The lightly proffered laurel,
> The easy, ungrudged praise.
> Comes now, to search your manhood
> Through all the thankless years,
> Cold, edged with dear-bought wisdom,
> The judgment of your peers!

This poem, incidentally, was among the poems best known by American schoolchildren until about 1945. (The graying editors of *The Little, Brown Reader* speak from firsthand experience; they were required to memorize it.)

Today *race*—a word that many people gladly do without—seems acceptable only when given a biological sense. Thus, the *Encyclopaedia Britannica*, 15th ed. (1993), begins its entry thus: "*race*, biological grouping within the human species, distinguished or classified according to genetically transmitted differences." But things don't proceed easily. Two paragraphs later we hear some uneasiness: "The overwhelming majority of all human populations can be separated into 6 to 10 large groupings known as geographic races, which correspond to geographic areas of continental proportions." Well, "the overwhelming majority" still omits some people, and "6 to 10" implies considerable uncertainty.

Later in the *Britannica* article we hear about such "racial variations" as skin pigmentation, hair texture and color, blood composition, and fingerprints.

> Through the process of evolution by natural selection, those characteristics endure that best enable their owners to function in their environments. Thus, most racial traits have demonstrable adaptive usefulness in the climates and conditions in which they originated. For instance, the blood condition called sickle-cell anemia affects mainly people of African descent; in its carrier state it protects against malaria, which is endemic in the hot, damp regions of Africa. The narrow noses of desert-dwelling Arabs humidify the dry air they inhale better than would shorter or broader noses.

Notice that the *Britannica* cautiously says only that "most" racial traits are functional; to the best of our knowledge, no one has convincingly argued that the differences in certain features, such as hair texture or lip form, can be explained functionally.

The *Britannica* article goes on to emphasize biology, then makes the point that "There are no pure races; all racial groups currently existing are thoroughly mixed," and it goes on to say that talk about language groups (the Aryan race), national groups (the Scottish race), and religious groups (the Jewish race) is "biologically and scientifically meaningless."

Obviously there are physical variations around the world, but *race* is now said to be a social or cultural construction. Why? Because (1) people of all races are more alike than they are different; (2) more variation exists within a given race as we think of it than exists, on average, between racial groups; and (3) migrations have made "pure" races almost nonexistent.

The Columbia Encyclopedia
Race (p. 263)

We chose this account, rather than the accounts in the *Britannica* or the *Americana* encyclopedias, because it is short, but an effective assignment can ask students to compare the *Columbia* account with one or both of the others. Students will learn that although encyclopedias supposedly convey only the facts, the accounts can be very different. They pretty much agree, however, in deploring any belief that race has anything to do with intelligence or personality traits. If one looks at old accounts, say, the famous 11th edition of the *Britannica* (1911), one finds this or that dark-skinned nation described as "childlike" and "given to indolence," or "crafty," etc. (We cannot cite passages at the moment, but we do recall encountering such passages.) All of the current accounts that we have read recognize genetic differences but insist that (in the words of *Columbia*) "the genes responsible for the hereditary differences between humans are few when compared with the vast number of genes common to all human beings regardless of the race to which they belong," deplore racism (*Columbia* speaks of "the vicious racial doctrines of Nazi Germany" and says, "This same approach complicated the integration movement in the United States"), and scrupulously avoid talking about the differences in intelligence and character that were taken for granted a century earlier.

Sharon Begley
Three Is Not Enough (p. 265)

The writer of this paragraph knows nothing about evolution, but she does have a question, and perhaps it is worth asking some students to do research on the issue. Begley says (paragraph 9) that "the long noses of North Africans and northern Europeans reveal that they evolved in dry or cold climates (the nose moistens air before the air reaches the lungs, and longer noses moisten more air)." If this is so, why don't Tibetans have long noses?

Begley's title, "Three Is Not Enough," and her final paragraph (she asks why we sort people "into so few groups"), suggest that we need additional categories. Perhaps, but some people suggest that we need fewer. See the first question suggested below.

Topics for Critical Thinking and Writing

1. If you are a native-born citizen of the United States, and you are asked to indicate your race, would you seriously consider responding "human"? And if asked your ethnicity, might you say "American"? Explain your response.

2. There is considerable talk about using "biracial" as a census classification. What arguments for and against such a category can you offer? Why, by the way, should the government be concerned with "race"?

Shelby Steele
Hailing While Black (p. 270)

We find Shelby Steele's writing elegant and precise, but it is also a bit terse. In order to require students to slow down and reread parts of the article, question 3, which we pose at the conclusion of the Casebook on Race (p. 277), asks for restatements of some of Steele's major points. Here are our own brief responses.

Racial profiling is the selection of a person to question or detain on the basis of race, usually on suspicion of criminal activity. Racial profiling is always considered by the person questioned or detained demeaning and prejudicial. The existence of racial profiling supports the demands of liberals ("the left") for additional powers for federal and state government to add laws and regulations to counter racism. Conservatives ("the right"), on the other hand, who countenance racial profiling because they favor restraining government intervention, seem unfair or unsympathetic. In his last sentence Steele suggests that he saw the event he recounted in his opening paragraph—hailing a cab in Manhattan—as a test of his conservatism, and he is unhappy that he sees such events as part of what he calls "America's ongoing culture war" (paragraph 1).

Steele's title, "Hailing While Black," is, of course, ironic. It takes off on the common expression "Driving While Black"—the experience of black drivers who may be pulled over by police for minor (or no) infractions of the law, having their persons and cars searched, etc. The term echoes the serious offense of Driving While under the Influence [of alcohol].

Question 8, following the Casebook on Race, proposes an essay on racial profiling. Depending on the class, it can also be useful to promote class discussion.

Randall Kennedy
Blind Spot (p. 272)

In his essay, Kennedy offers a clear exposition of the arguments of both the supporters and the opponents of racial profiling in law enforcement. What makes his essay particularly interesting is his argument that both supporters and opponents of racial profiling reveal inconsistencies when they turn their attention to affirmative action: the supporters of racial profiling oppose affirmative action while the opponents support it. His explanation of their inconsistencies is lucid and persuasive.

Kennedy does not reveal his own position on either racial profiling or affirmative action. Instead he recommends that the two camps he has discussed and analyzed should listen to each other. In other words, he proposes a Rogerian argument. (See *LBR* pp. 73–78).

A good place to begin discussion of Kennedy's essay is to ask: To what does Kennedy's title "Blind Spot" refer?

Students can be asked to discuss, or to write about, the positions that Rodriguez takes on affirmitave action (in his interview, p. 245) and Steele on racial profiling (p. 270), and to compare what they each say to Kennedy's views.

Stanley Crouch
Race Is Over (p. 274)

"Multiculturalism" and "identity politics"—in such forms as "African-American" and "Asian-American"—are talked about so much today that some students can hardly conceive of the old days when Theodore Roosevelt could say, to great applause, "There is no room in this country for hyphenated Americanism." One might even cite a more recent passage envisioning a color-blind view of Americans (quoted in our Short Views), Martin Luther King Jr.'s "I have a dream that my four little children will one day live in a nation where they will not be judged by the color of their skin but by the content of their character."

Of course, there is nothing inconsistent between King's dream and the multiculturalist's insistence that cultures other than Anglo culture should be valued and preserved in the United States. Or at least such is our view; but what concerns you is your view and the views of your students. In paragraph 7 Crouch talks about assimilation, and we imagine that a good topic for discussion will be this sentence of his: "We look at so-called 'assimilation' as some form of oppression, some loss of identity, even a way of 'selling out.'" (*The American Heritage Dictionary*, third edition, defines assimilation thus: "The process whereby a minority group gradually adopts the customs and attitudes of the prevailing culture.") Why, students might be asked, should an individual not be free to choose his or her culture? Obviously no one thinks twice if an American of, say, German Protestant descent, or of French Catholic descent, has no special interest in Germany or France and subscribes to what we can roughly call Anglo values. As several sociologists have pointed out, by the middle of the twentieth century Jews and Irish Catholics had become "white," i.e., for the most part they were not seen as "different" from white Protestants. But assimilation is obviously much more difficult for persons whose ancestry goes back to Asia or Africa. These people are easily *seen* as "different," whatever their cultural patterns. On the other hand, we all know persons of African or Asian origin whose culture seems uninfluenced by their remote past. But the strong interest in ethnicity has generated the terms "oreo" and "banana," used to deride African Americans and Asian Americans who allegedly think like Anglos.

But need our color determine the values that we subscribe to, or the kind of person we want to become? No one thinks it strange if a WASP or a Jew becomes a professor of Greek literature or of Chinese art. Why, then, cannot an Asian American become deeply interested in Greek drama? Or an African American become deeply interested in Chinese language and literature? Why is such a person scorned as someone who is disloyal to his or her origins? For a fairly short provocative discussion of *assimilation,* students can be referred to the article with that title, written by Stephen H. Sumida, in *A Companion to American Thought* (1995), ed. Richard Wrightman Fox and James T. Kloppenberg. Sumida, by the way, cites the example of the black poet Countee Cullen, who often wrote about the experience of being black in the United States but who as a poet saw himself chiefly in the tradition of the Elizabethan lyric poets and of John Keats. Cullen did *not* think he always had to write about being black, and to the best of our knowledge he never wrote in the black vernacular. (It happens that the Cullen poem we use in this chapter is indeed about a black in a white world, but the form [quatrains] is a traditional English form.)

Countee Cullen
Incident (p. 278)

The poem seems to be of the utmost simplicity: twelve lines without any figures of speech and without any obscure words. But it has its complexities, beginning with the title.

Our first question in the text asks students to think about the word "incident." It's our impression that an "incident" is usually a minor affair—something detached from what comes before and after, of little consequence. For instance: "During the banquet a waiter dropped a tray full of dishes, but apart from this incident the affair was a great success." There are, of course, plenty of exceptions, such as the famous "Incident at Harpers Ferry," but we think that on the whole an incident is (1) minor and (2) a distinct occurrence.

Cullen's title therefore is ironic—the episode might seem to be minor, but in fact it has left an indelible mark on the speaker's mind (and on the minds of countless readers). And since it continues to have its effect, it is not something separate and done with. The apparent simplicity, then, of the title and of the entire poem, is deceptive since this seemingly trivial and unconnected episode stands for, or embodies, an enormous force in American life.

It's a good idea to ask a student to read the poem aloud in class (true for all poems, of course), so that students can hear the rhythms. On the whole, "Incident" sounds like a happy jingle, but of course that is part of the irony. Two details that strike us as especially effective are the enjambments in lines 7 and 11.

Of the other ten lines, eight end with some mark of punctuation, and the other two ("I saw a Baltimorean" and "I saw the whole of Baltimore") could be complete in themselves. But in the seventh line we are propelled into the horrible event of the eighth line ("And so I smiled, but he poked out / His tongue, and called me, 'Nigger'"); and in the eleventh line we are propelled into the final line, the line that tells us that this whole "incident" was by no means trivial ("Of all the things that happened there / That's all that I remember").

Studies of Countee Cullen include: Helen J. Dinger, *A Study of Countee Cullen* (1953); Stephen H. Brontz, *Roots of Negro Racial Consciousness—The 1920s: Three Harlem Renaissance Authors* (1954); Blanche E. Ferguson, *Countee Cullen and the Negro Renaissance* (1966); and Margaret Perry, *A Bio-Bibliography of Countee P. Cullen* (1969).

Instructors will find these secondary sources helpful, but none of them offers help on one issue that will be in the air when Cullen's poem is discussed. "Nigger," in line 8, is an ugly, offensive word—which is central to Cullen's point in the poem, but which is nonetheless a hard word for the teacher and for students to say aloud and to analyze.

We know some instructors who press hard on the word "Nigger" in class: they want the students to feel very vividly the crude bigotry and shock of the term. This approach, we confess, does not work for us, and so we follow a different path. Often, after we have read the poem and begun to examine it with students, we have paused to say outright that it's hard to use and talk about offensive racial and ethnic slurs and epithets. Yes, one of them is in Cullen's poem, and thus it has to be considered as essential to its meaning. But, still, we tell and teach ourselves that such words are wrong—that they should not be used, ever, because they are offensive—and thus it cuts against our principles and (we hope) our practice to hear ourselves voicing them.

This may or may not be the best approach, but at the least it acknowledges for students that *something* is awry and uncomfortable in the room when the instructor and students start using the word "Nigger" or other words like it. Keep in mind what the students are or might be thinking and feeling. Talk about it. The tone of the class will be better, we believe, if you are sensitive to this issue and seek as best you can to address it carefully. The mistake would be to assume that, in a classroom context, ugly, offensive words will be heard by students neutrally, dispassionately.

8

TEACHING AND LEARNING

Illustrations

Winslow Homer
Blackboard (p. 280)

Students who know Homer only through *The Gulf Stream* or perhaps from his pictures of hunters and fishermen may be surprised by Homer's *Blackboard,* but he painted a fair number of images of women. What may be especially surprising even to people who have more than a superficial knowledge of Homer is the very evident concern with composition—with geometry, we might say.

We are not speaking only of the images on the blackboard, which, we learn from Nicolai Cikovsky Jr. and Franklin Kelly's *Winslow Homer* (1995), show instruction in drawing as part of industrial education. Of course, all artists are interested in arrangements of lines, in composition, and almost any formal analysis of any picture will involve saying things like "The horse's neck echoes the curve of the fountain," or "The line of the arm parallels the branch of the tree." Artists indeed organize their work, often thinking in accordance with geometry. One thinks of such famous comments as "Treat Nature in terms of the cylinder, the sphere, the cone, all in perspective" (Cézanne); "Every group must form a pyramid" (Mengs); "Composition is the art of arranging in a decorative manner the various elements at the painter's disposal for the expression of his feelings" (Matisse); and "[While painting a portrait the artist at work thinks], 'This new brick is a little too heavy and to my mind puts too much weight on the left; I must add a good-sized counterweight on the right to restore equilibrium'" (Klee). But in *Blackboard* Homer goes beyond what artists do when they structure a painting. He seems to be playfully designing a picture that echoes the principles being taught: the lower edge of the blackboard divides the picture almost at the middle (admittedly the upper portion is a trifle larger); if one draws a vertical line down the center of the picture, it passes through the young woman's nose; if one considers the three horizontal panels, the relationship from top to bottom is, roughly, 3, 2, 1; the measurement from the top of the blackboard to the top of the picture is pretty much the same as the measurement from the bottom of the wall to the bottom of the picture.

Where have we seen a late-nineteenth-century American picture that is composed so lucidly? Answer: in Whistler's *Arrangement in Grey and Black,* better known as *Whistler's Mother,* where the human figure, also in profile, is treated as one form among others, in this case the other forms being a curtain that hangs at the left and a picture on the wall between the drapery and the sitter. The very fact that each figure is in profile is significant, for a profile offers the spectator the opportunity to examine an interesting contour, far more interesting than the contours of a frontal view. Frontal views and three-quarter views are fine if the artist wants to reveal character—think of Rembrandt's portraits, or, for that matter, of Grant Wood's *American Gothic*—but profiles are better suited to the artist who is emphasizing pattern. Incidentally, Homer (1836–1910) and Whistler (1834–1903) were close contemporaries, and the two pictures are fairly close in date (*Arrangement*, 1871; *Blackboard*, 1877).

The picture is rightly called *Blackboard*; if it were called *The Teacher*, honesty would require us to say that this teacher seems to have very little contact with her pupils. But taking a cue from Whistler's title, we might think of this picture as *Arrangement of Lines*.

Ron James
The Lesson—Planning a Career (p. 281)

This photograph, apparently of a class in an adult education program, is saddening. The teacher is not shown and we may thus infer that little significant teaching is going on. In any case, of the three students, at least two seem to be less than rapt in whatever they are doing, and all three are, literally, up against the wall. The wall itself is hauntingly blank except for the wavering legend, "Wages, careers and colleges." The letters of these words were apparently fastened uncertainly even at the start, and by the time someone got to "colleges" either the glue gave out or the letters were improperly glued and they fell off, for now they are held (not very attractively) by bits of transparent tape. Somehow one doesn't quite believe that the "Wages, careers and colleges" will be forthcoming for most of the students in this program.

Short Views

Topics for Critical Thinking and Writing

1. If you find Goodman's proposal appealing, explain why you do. If you find his proposal or part of his argument untenable, explain why. (*Note:* It is possible that you will find his argument both appealing and untenable. Explain both points concisely in one to three paragraphs.) What do you think is (or should be) the purpose of high schools?

2. Diederich points out that some teachers teach badly. Drawing on your own experience, indicate in what ways your teachers of writing could have taught better.

3. To what extent does Diederich's description of his students' experience learning to write reflect your own experience? Or, in an essay of 500 to 750 words, describe, analyze, and evaluate your education thus far in how to write.

4. Evaluate, as an argument, the analogy in Goldman's first two paragraphs. Is it reasonable? Is it persuasive?

Plato
The Myth of the Cave (p. 287)

The form of the dialogue, of course, has a dramatic effectiveness (we see and hear the give and take), but it is also a philosophic device: we arrive at a truth by asking questions and answering them, or by having other people try to answer them. In a dialogue, the problem is studied from more than one point of view, not simply to add opinion on top of opinion but to refute irrational points of view, thereby coming to a rational resolution. Moreover, this method (for the dialogues are imitations of Socrates's dialectic method) assumes that teaching is not so much a matter of pouring ideas into an empty head as it is a matter of drawing out ideas that are dormant in the soul. Perhaps one of the grandest things that Socrates taught through his dialectic method was that we can find answers ourselves if we are skeptical of authority and if we ask ourselves questions.

We have spoken of a rational resolution, and of course when one thinks of Plato (or of Socrates) one thinks of reason. But one also thinks of Plato's occasional myths, such as "The Myth of the Cave" (hence question 5). These myths work, we might say, poetically; they supplement rational discourse by providing us with images that make us see and feel. Take, as a simple example, the passage almost at the start of this extract: Socrates asks Glaucon to imagine chained prisoners in a cave, looking at shadows, and Glaucon is moved—as we are—to say, "You have shown me a strange image, and they are strange prisoners." Socrates's cool but startling response is, "Like ourselves." Here we are not convinced rationally; surely we feel as well as see.

Question 3, on the painfulness involved in learning, can be related effectively to Toni Cade Bambara's story "The Lesson" in *LBR*, p. 366, where Sylvia experiences pain and shows irritation.

About question 6, concerning metaphoric uses of light as intellectual comprehension: in addition to "enlighten" and "illuminate" and "see," the following expressions are relevant: "to throw light on a subject," "to clarify," "to clear up," "it dawned on me," "I had a bright idea."

Topic for Critical Thinking and Writing

According to "The Myth of the Cave," what emotions do the unenlightened prisoners feel? What emotions do the freed people feel? (We want students to notice that the prisoners compete for "honors and glories" and "fight with one another about shadows only." These prisoners—with the complacency of ignorance—ridicule the enlightened person. Note, too, that the enlightened person pities the prisoners but has no wish to go back into the cave to enlighten them. Our point: these characters are not flat abstractions but are indeed "like ourselves.")

Richard Wright
Writing and Reading (p. 294)

In the opening paragraph of this excerpt from *Black Boy* Wright recalls his days in the eighth grade. He was "more conscious" of himself, "bored, wondering, dreaming." Students empathize with these emotions and can be asked how they countered them. Some focused on sports, almost all on daydreams about sex; a few responded as Wright did by writing stories. But it is a rare student who experienced the opposition to his or her writing that Wright experienced. His accomplishment (seeing his story in a black newspaper) distances him still further from his classmates and antagonizes his granny, his aunt and uncle, and worries even his mother. But the encouragement from the newspaper editor proved pivotal, and Wright begins to dream "of going north and writing books, novels." He begins to understand that it wasn't just the people he knew who distrusted his talent, it was "the entire educational system of the South," which was supported by the state of Mississippi and by southern senators. He was yearning for "a mode of being" "upon which the penalty of death had been placed." It is worth noting in class that "the penalty of death" was no exaggeration. Students who are unaware of what life for African Americans in the south was like a few decades ago need only to read the brief article on "lynching" in the *Columbia Encyclopedia* (between 1882 and 1968 some 3,440 black men and women were lynched, primarily for "outspokenness" and other offenses against whites) or research lynching on the Web.

And the rest of the excerpt demonstrates Wright's need for caution as he attempts to borrow books from the public library. He was, of course, not permitted to borrow them for himself—he had to consider carefully which white man would be willing to assist him, and he pretended to be illiterate with the librarian.

Two of the Topics for Critical Thinking and Writing make especially good writing assignments. The first asks students to compare their own use of a public library with Wright's; the third topic asks students to summarize a passage of dialogue in "Writing and Reading" and then to analyze what has been gained or lost. Some students, particularly international students, have had personal experiences of opposition to their quests for education and can be encouraged to write about what the opposition was and how they dealt with it.

Richard Rodriguez
Public and Private Language (p. 305)

Although Rodriguez regrets the effects in his family life of his learning English in school, he is clear that education in the United States ought to be in English. It was through learning English (in the first grade) that he acquired the "public identity" which is "the great lesson of school." The lesson required a visit to his home by nuns, and it required his parents (despite their limitations with the language) to speak English to him and to his brother and sister. It required also his loss of the sense that Spanish was a "private language" and English a "public language." Moving to English meant that he was gradually abandoning the "pleasing family life" which had been conducted in Spanish. But by seven, he was convinced that he was indeed an American citizen (which he had, of course, been since birth). He now owned the "public identity" but had lost "the golden age" of his childhood.

Rodriguez does not argue the merits of learning English in school or of using English to learn other subjects. He explores the difficulties of the choice while assuming that the choice was correct. But many students from immigrant families will have had other experiences; it is useful to draw these students out. Rodriquez describes a Catholic school with nuns who visit home and with daily tutoring in English. Did your students have such experiences? Or was their elementary and even high school education conducted partly or largely in their own language? Do they feel, as Rodriguez clearly does, that their education was worthwhile?

Maya Angelou
Graduation (p. 310)

Many students do not perceive that the elevated or heroic diction of the first part (for example, "glorious release," "nobility," "like travelers with exotic destinations," all from the first paragraph) is an essential prelude to the descent in the middle ("It was awful to be Negro"). Neither do these students see the comedy, mixed of course with pathos, in such a passage as "My academic work was among the best of the year. I could say the preamble to the Constitution even faster than Bailey." Nor, often, do they see the comedy in paragraph 29. "We stood," "we sat," "we rose again," "we remained standing for a brief minute before the choir director and the principal signaled to us, rather desperately I thought, to take our seats." Nor do they always realize, even after finishing the essay, that this confusion about sitting and standing resulted from the deletion of the Negro national anthem, presumably out of deference to the white speaker. The difficult thing about teaching this essay, then, is showing some students that they missed a good part of an essay that they read with ease and believed they fully understood. Probably they miss some of the comedy because they can scarcely believe that an essay on graduation can be even partly amusing—unless it is an out-and-out spoof.

We try, then, in teaching this chapter from *I Know Why the Caged Bird Sings*, to help students see the difference between the youthful (and, from an adult's point of view, touching yet amusing) excitement and confidence of the beginning, and the mature, partly understated knowledge of the final three paragraphs. In this narration of the movement from innocence to experience, the last paragraph is especially tight-lipped and tough-minded, with its "if we were a people much given to revealing secrets," "slavery cured us of that weakness," and "it may be enough, however. . . ."

Topics for Critical Thinking and Writing

1. Question 3 following the essay can be used as an assignment for writing one paragraph; question 2 for a brief essay, two to four paragraphs.

2. Narrate an experience that disclosed a lesson of some value to you. (Students should be cautioned not to look exclusively at momentous events in their lives or to expect to make startling discoveries. Most of us can, on reflection, recall experiences from which we learned—however dimly we perceived the lesson at the time—something that was and continues to be of value to us.)

3. Write an essay titled "From Innocence to Experience—A Comparison of 'Graduation' and 'The Lesson'" (Toni Cade Bambara's "The Lesson," in *LBR*, p. 366).

Neil Postman
Order in the Classroom (p. 320)

Because we graying editors of *The Little, Brown Reader* were in our childhood educated by teachers who, for the most part, ran a tight ship (boys wore neckties, and students stood when called on), we can only vaguely comprehend any other kind of schooling for young people. Still, we are a bit uneasy with Postman's essay, partly because good sense is mixed with mere crankiness. For instance, take this passage in paragraph 21:

> A young man who goes through the day with a radio affixed to his ear is learning to be indifferent to any shared sound. A young woman who can turn off a television program that does not suit her needs at the moment is learning impatience with any stimulus that is not responsive to her interests.

The point about the headsets seems to us worth contemplation, but what about the point about television? Should the young lady learn patience by refraining from switching off a television program that bores her? Surely there are many programs that deserve to be switched off. Furthermore, even in the good old days of radio and books, we could always switch off the radio or close the book. Still, having said this, we want to repeat that we think Postman's essay deserves discussion.

Topic for Critical Thinking and Writing

In paragraph 24 Postman questions the judgment of those who disagree with him. Evaluate this argument.

Robert Coles
On Raising Moral Children (p. 326)

Coles evidently defines moral intelligence as consisting of the capacities for goodness, for kindness, and the awareness of the needs of others. He suggests that children acquire moral intelligence, first of all, through attention to their parents. Children are, he says "attentive witness[es] of grown-up morality." But he goes beyond suggesting that children imitate their parents. He tells a series of anecdotes to reveal the process by which children acquire morality. In the fifth paragraph he quotes a mother who says, "I think we start sending signals to our kids from Day One," and tells the story of Maisie and her six-month-old infant, who tossed his bottle from his high chair. Maisie's behavior "started teaching her son right versus wrong—how he should behave, and what he shouldn't do." Coles's next anecdote is about a six-year-old boy (elementary school children become "intensely moral" creatures) whose interest in a telescope translates into interest in human behavior. He next tells of his conversations with a depressed adolescent. The point here is that by revealing something of his own life as an adolescent, he demonstrates interest in his patient that prompts his recovery. His last anecdote concerns a Harvard student who angrily asks, "Well, how do you teach people to be good?" Books and classroom discussions help, Coles asserts, but the chief ingredient of goodness is a commitment to be kind, and here he uses the metaphor of sailing to indicate something about kindness (we're not sure what it is) but, more likely, to end his essay on an evocative note.

These anecdotes have been chronologically arranged. But the first anecdote, which occurs in his third and fourth paragraphs, concerns his son, whom Coles was rushing to the hospital following the son's injury. The point of this anecdote is, we believe, that children not only learn morality from grownups but also that grownups have something to learn from children. In our opinion, this anecdote, which shifts the point a bit but adds to the discussion, would have made a more fitting conclusion to the essay than the sailing metaphor, which places Coles's analysis in the doldrums.

Mary Field Belenky et al.
How Women Learn (p. 331)

Women's Ways of Knowing: The Development of Self, Voice and Mind (1986), the book from which we excerpt these pages, is a study of how women learn and how the institutions of schools and families "both promote and hinder women's development" (p. 4). The study, based on extensive interviews with 135 women, explores experiences that affected either the women's changing concepts of self or their intellectual development. Often the same experiences affected both, feelings of self-worth and learning ability being intertwined.

Our excerpt is from Chapter 9 of the book, in which the authors report on the academic experiences of the ninety women in their study who were enrolled in one of six academic institutions. The institutions varied widely (included among them were an "Ivy League" women's college, an inner-city community college, and an alternative urban public high school), but all of the women were, the authors tell us, "ordinary women . . . neither teachers nor scholars nor even feminists but simply students." And other similarities were to emerge across the spectrum of "age, social class, ethnicity, and academic achievement" (p. 193).

In this part of the interview, each subject was asked about "good and bad teachers, good and bad assignments, good and bad programs or courses," and whether participation in the academic program had "changed the way she thought about herself or the world." Finally, each woman was asked, "Looking back over your whole life, can you tell us about a really powerful learning experience that you've had, in or out of school?" Despite the diversity of experiences recalled, the authors report that "some common themes emerged, themes that are distinctively, although surely not exclusively, feminine" (p. 191).

The theme that unites the two anecdotes is the need of both women for assurance of their intellectual competence (the demonstration performed by the philosophy teacher provided powerful assurance). The authors go further. In the last paragraph they state emphatically that their interviews convinced them that all women, regardless of background or achievement, need to know that they are "capable of intelligent thought."

Our questions following the text direct students to its main points while trying to elicit their own experiences as well as reactions to the text. In class we also discuss the effective use of narrative in making a point, particularly an arguable one, and the equally effective use of exposition in focusing the reader's attention on the point the writer wants the narrative to make.

To answer the questions:

1. The science professor is characterized first by the verb that announces his entrance: he "marched into the lecture hall." And as if his self-assurance alone were not enough to intimidate (and alienate), we are told that he "smiled a thin, dry smile" as he "*revealed* the correct answer" (emphasis added). Lest we think that the seventeen-year-old girl whose "sense of herself as a knower was shaky" was simply a wimp (she promptly abandons not only the course but also all hope of ever understanding science), we are advised by the first sentence that the stories we're about to hear are of "two *ordinary* women" (emphasis added). In other words, we should find nothing remarkable about this student's reaction; all women, at least, can empathize with her.

2. The stories are both, of course, about young, impressionable women; both stories involve an academic discipline being introduced through a classroom demonstration. And both stories are, importantly, about power and empowerment. The ways in which the stories contrast on this last point are clearly outlined in paragraphs 5–8. The chief difference is that the science professor leaves the student feeling dependent, powerless, and stupid ("small and scared"). The philosophy professor's demonstration, on the other hand, assured the student that she already possessed the one credential she needed to enter the discipline of philosophy: her own intelligence.

   Is it a relevant difference, or simply an accident, that the science teacher (the intimidating authority) is male while the nurturing philosophy teacher is female?

3. Most students will argue that science is about "indisputable facts" and the "real world"; the science teacher knows the facts and has the answers; the students are there to learn them. In literature courses and probably in phi-

losophy too, it's all a matter of your opinion. And to some extent, despite the caricature, students who say these things have a point. In the physical sciences, despite the enormous mysteries of the universe we inhabit and the inconsistencies among current theories about it (for example, between the theory of relativity and quantum mechanics), there are currently accepted bodies of knowledge, theory, and procedural methods. Novices must learn them. In addition, most sciences are taught—need to be taught—sequentially. An advanced course in quantum theory requires prior study of at least introductory courses in physics and mathematics. By contrast, there is far less agreement about what a student of literature should know or how the student should proceed. In an introductory course she might read a play by Shakespeare, a novel by Toni Morrison, poems by Emily Dickinson and Wallace Stevens, or all of the above. That is, although by and large the more one reads the better one is likely to read, a student can begin reading almost anywhere; it is not necessary first to study literary history, or chronology, or to start with something "easy." And although theories of literature abound, there is no agreed-upon methodology for studying literature or creating it. Philosophy as a discipline is probably closer to literature on most of these points than it is to science.

Students often suppose, even in literature courses, that there is a "right answer" or a "correct interpretation." Often enough their instructors must resist the temptation to behave like the authoritarian figures (mischievously concealing the right answers) that their students believe them to be. And of course one finds science teachers who successfully engage their students in a process of discovery and still manage to teach as much science as their colleagues who lecture to "cover the material." But given the accepted bodies of knowledge and theory in the sciences (what Thomas Kuhn has termed "paradigms") and the prerequisites for advanced study, introductory courses in the sciences are, in our opinion (and in our students' experiences), more likely to be taught according to a more authoritarian model than courses in literature or philosophy.

4.   The concluding paragraph argues that to thrive in academic institutions, women students need to be taught that they are "capable of intelligent thought." (Differences on this point between the ways men and women learn are implied.)

The book as a whole argues that academic institutions, having been designed by men to teach male students, do not adequately serve the needs of female students. Further, when pedagogical methods are examined and evaluated, the students who serve first as subjects and then as models have been, until recently, male students. Male-centered pedagogy tends to be adversarial. The student is challenged. He is taught to challenge—to criticize, debate, evaluate—the opinions, ideas, and values of others and ultimately his own preconceived ideas and prejudices. Critical thinking, as the process is sometimes labeled, enables the student to construct arguments that can stand up to the judgment of impersonal rules and authorities. This epistemological orientation is called "separate knowing," a term the authors borrow from Carol Gilligan (*In A Different Voice: Psychological Theory and Women's Development*, Harvard University Press, 1982). "Separate knowing" leaves many women feeling uncomfortable, excluded, inauthentic, or stupid. "Connected knowing," a term coined by Belenky et al. in *Women's Ways of Knowing,* as a result of their investigation, is more congenial to women. It entails understanding a position rather than challenging it, reciprocity rather than mastery, collaboration rather than autonomy. "Connected knowing" values intuition and experience, the personal over the impersonal. Although the authors disclaim that separate and connected knowing are "gender-specific" they hypothesize that "more women than men tip toward connected knowing and more men than women toward separate knowing" (p. 103). It is our impression that when they write of "women's ways of knowing," it is "connected knowing" that they have chiefly in mind. And they argue that until "women's ways of knowing," which have been generally neglected and even denigrated, are recognized and valued, women students will continue to be undermined and their intellectual achievements hindered.

(Our brief summary does not, of course, do justice to this richly detailed and subtly persuasive book. But the summary may help instructors elicit from students, male and female, experiences that tend to confirm or deny differences between men and women as students and as learners.)

Topics for Critical Thinking and Writing

1.   Recount an experience, in school or out, that powerfully affected your performance or confidence in yourself as a student.

2.   Looking back over your experience, do you find any evidence that female students are less confident than male students, or have different ways of approaching new material, or are treated differently by their teachers? Write an essay explaining your ideas, in part by recounting the chief experience or experiences that helped you to formulate them. You may want to frame your essay as a response to "How Women Learn."

Fan Shen
The Classroom and the Wider Culture: Identity as a Key to Learning English Composition (p. 334)

In writing classes in English, what was difficult for Fan Shen were the instructions to "be yourself" and to "write what you think." These instructions embodied "a social and cultural experience." In China, "I" had been subordinated to "we"—of the working class, the Party, the country. "I" would have seemed "disrespectful" of the Communist Party or, in scholarship, "boastful." Shen needed also to learn a Western critical system. In China, one learned to approach a topic in a leisurely way, from the outside in, or to practice "yijing," that is, to create pictures while reading. To learn the Western system meant not only to learn new meanings for words like "I" or "individualism" but also to forge a new identity.

Shen hoped "The Classroom and the Wider Culture" would help college instructors who teach students from China, Korea, Vietnam, or India. We think that it will. But we're more interested in having students recently from those countries read Shen's lucid account of his own struggles to understand the new instructions and to form a new identity. We also hope that students who grow up in the United States will understand Shen's struggles and, we believe, understand their own struggles. "To be yourself" and "to write what you think" are new experiences for all of us as we learn to focus on intellectual problems and to write about them.

David Gelernter
Unplugged (p. 344)

The essay strikes us as readable and highly provocative; we think it will make for a lively class period.

The comments in paragraphs 4–5, on multimedia and Shakespeare, especially interest us. Gelernter is distressed that "You don't just *read* Shakespeare; you watch actors performing, listen to songs, view Elizabethan buildings." But this, of course, is exactly what Shakespeare's contemporaries did. They went to the theater (saw a building) and watched actors perform the plays on a stage. Moreover, the plays contained songs; the audience did not read the songs but actually heard them sung. Why, then, is it a bad thing for students to experience the play somewhat as the Elizabethans did? Of course, we now say that Shakespeare's plays are not only drama but are also literature; they can be experienced—in valuable ways—through books, as well as in the theater. We understand the gist of Gelernter's point, but we think he chose a poor example. A better example would be a novel—a real book, such as *Wuthering Heights*—versus a video version of it, which, we assume, would necessarily be reductive.

And what about hypermedia, the subject of paragraph 6? Like Gelernter, we sometimes are distressed by materials that keep the eye jumping around. We especially have in mind those textbooks with boxes and sidebars that look like *Time* magazine. *Why*, we wonder, can't the author of the book just let the readers move along steadily, instead of inviting them to start this part, then jump to that, and then to a third thing? And certainly we agree with Gelernter that "teaching children to understand the orderly unfolding of a plot or a logical argument is a crucial part of education." But we also strongly feel that students should learn that there is not only one way in which to develop an argument—or a plot. When one sits down to write, one usually finds that there are several or even many ways of going about the task. After a good deal of exploring (revising), one produces a version, but always with the awareness that it well might have been different. Yes, the final work has a structure, or ought to have one, but the structure is not inevitable, and in fact it may lend a false sense of inevitability, of finality. The apparently seamless garment may perhaps be undone if a reader dares to pull at a thread, e.g., dares to question the writer's unstated assumptions or looks at the problem from a different angle.

Paragraph 8 touches on "allow me" programs, e.g., spell checkers. Here we think we can speak with some authority. Like Gelernter, we find a spell checker handy, chiefly for catching typos but also for catching misspellings. Of course, if one is unsure how to spell a word, one usually goes to the desk dictionary, and perhaps browses among the meanings and the etymology and thus learns a good deal, but the spell checker is especially useful because it calls to our attention words that we mistakenly think we know how to spell and that we would not dream of looking up in a dictionary. *Example:* Not until we had seen many winters go by, i.e., not until we used a spell checker, did we learn that the proper spelling is *supersede*, not *supercede*. On the other hand, we have no firsthand experience of programs that supposedly assist writers to improve their style. Our guess, based on what we have heard, is that they don't do much good, but they don't do any harm. It will be interesting to hear students talk about such programs.

Topics for Critical Thinking and Writing

1. If you used computers in your elementary or secondary school, evaluate their contribution to your education. (This need not be an all-or-nothing issue; it may be that computers were useless in some courses, moderately useful in others, and highly useful in still others.)

2. One of Gelernter's complaints (paragraph 3) is that "computers discount words in favor of pictures and pictures in favor of video." Is this true—and if it is true, is it necessarily a bad thing? Explain.

3. Paragraph 9 touches on whether "drilling addition and subtraction in an age of calculators is a waste of time." Your views?

Bibliographic note: Todd Oppenheimer, "The Computer Delusion," *Atlantic Monthly* (July 1997):45–63, pretty much takes Gelernter's line. Oppenheimer argues that there is no evidence that computers significantly improve learning, and that they may in fact be having a harmful influence because schools that turn to computers often cut programs in the arts in order to make room for computers. The October 1997 issue of *Atlantic* prints responses (pp. 10 and 14) to Oppenheimer's essay.

Hubert B. Herring
On the Eve of Extinction: Four Years of High School (p. 347)

If you assign this selection, you may want to ask students, when you assign it, to think about two questions concerning the audience: For whom is it written? How do you know?

The first clue, evident even before reading the piece, is the place of publication: it appeared in the *New York Times,* an organ more likely to be read by parents than by high school students. And even a cursory reading indicates that it is written by a father, writing to other parents rather than to high school students. The fifth paragraph contains a little joke: "One senior of my acquaintance (he shall remain anonymous; otherwise I'll never get him to clean up his room) recently managed to extend lunch to three full school periods." Herring's readers, i.e., other parents, smile and nod knowingly; they have also had trouble getting kids to clean up their rooms. Paragraph 8 is more or less in this vein too, ending "So chill out, Dad."

The essay is partly a good read for parents, who are relieved to hear that they are not the only ones who are upset by the senioritis that afflicts their children. But is there also an argument in this essay? First, one would want to find out from students if they agree that the last semester in high school is a waste. They may take a different view, and they may support it with interesting evidence. Second, if they agree that Herring has called attention to a problem, they may or may not agree with one or both of his two solutions: get tough—or give up and make the sabbatical official.

In short, we think the essay lends itself to rhetorical study, especially concerning the author's relation to the imagined audience, and also to serious argument. The tone is genial, but Herring does offer arguments, and if there really is a problem, his solutions deserve to be evaluated.

Nadya Labi
Classrooms for Sale (p. 349)

Students ought to be able to bring relevant experiences to bear when they write about this essay—they either have or have not been exposed to the commercialism described, and they have or have not responded to the ads—and, perhaps more important, they ought to be able to take a position. They might argue, for instance, that, yes, the ads do have an effect, but so what? The revenue is needed, and if they drink Coke or buy Calvin Klein garb, no great harm is done. (*Not* our own position, we hasten to add—just an example.)

We don't doubt that "commercialism in classrooms has become . . . rampant" (see our third and fourth questions), but we are surprised to learn, from the article itself, that the references to brand names in the McGraw-Hill textbook were *not* paid for and are merely the result of an attempt by the authors to catch the attention of readers by the venerable device of being concrete, a device recommended by virtually every college textbook on composition.

The final paragraph speaks of the possibility of a McDonald's Middle School and a Coke High. This surely is a deliberately comic *reductio ad absurdum* (note the pun in "coke high"—the topic of our sixth question), but indeed where does one draw the line? It takes only a moment of reflection to recall that (a) hotshot college athletic teams wear garb that advertises a commercial product, and (b) some college buildings—maybe especially gymnasiums and auditoriums—are named for corporations. It's our impression, too, but we may be wrong, that some business schools have buildings (or parts of buildings such as auditoriums) named for corporate donors. Is it appropriate for colleges to name buildings after corporate donors but not appropriate for schools? If so, why?

Amy Tan
In the Canon, for All the Wrong Reasons (p. 352)

We begin class discussion with an analysis of the title. "Canon," which derives from a Greek word meaning measuring rod or rule, here refers to a body of works deemed worthy or authentic by literary critics or academics. Specifically, Tan's novels are in the canon of multicultural writings. "For All the Wrong Reasons" signals her wish to dismiss what she calls "this development." Several ironic references in her essay support this dismissal. In her first paragraph, for example, she refers to the (imagined) "Halls of Education" and asserts that "Multicultural Literature" is "also known in many schools as 'Required Reading.'" Although our students, in their speech, at any rate, are frequently ironic, they often fail to recognize irony in print. Pausing to examine Tan's irony can prove bracing.

In answer to our fifth question in the text, some students bring up "Nigger Jim" in *Huckleberry Finn,* and that can lead to an interesting discussion. Although Tan is reluctant to discuss her "intentions" in writing fiction, it might be worth speculating what Mark Twain's intentions were in creating Jim and perhaps contrasting that creation with "Pap."

Tan's thesis, we believe, occurs in her paragraph 21. "I write to discover the past for myself." We share Tan's view of writing as discovery and would like to convert our students to share it also. Writing an essay can be and should be an act of discovery. So we pause at this passage, and also at a sentence in her paragraph 22: "I also think of reading as an act of faith, a hope that I will discover something remarkable about ordinary life, about myself." Do our students share this hope? We hope so.

Dave Eggers
Serve or Fail (p. 356)

Eggers argues that colleges should consider instituting a service require-
ment for graduation. He supports his claim largely by an account of his own
experience as an undergraduate. He asserts that "college is too long—it
should be three years" (but offers no support for that claim). In addition to his
own experience, he offers an analysis of college students. They are, he writes:

- uniquely suited for service
- "less programmed" and "more mature" than high school students
- likely to benefit themselves from service to others

He would probably exempt community college students, and he proposes
academic credit for service. He further offers support for the service require-
ment from two authorities who apparently approve of it: a member of Penn-
sylvania's House of Representatives and the former Governor of California.

To answer our third question, we find Eggers's tone a bit off-putting. His
article is lively and sometimes amusing, but it is likely to alienate many readers, particularly college students, who almost universally believe that they
spend every waking moment studying and preparing for exams. Most of the
letters in response reflect the writers' distance from Eggers and his argument.

Topic for Critical Thinking and Writing

Write a letter of response to Eggers's "Serve or Fail."

Brent Staples
What Adolescents Miss When We Let Them
Grow Up in Cyberspace (p. 360)

Staples's account of his experience when he was fifteen "submitting to
the intense scrutiny" of the father of his "10th-grade heartthrob" is an engaging introduction to his argument. It prepares us for his indictment of adolescents' overuse of the Internet: for e-mail, chat rooms, instant messaging,
online shopping, and Web surfing. These activities, Staples contends, isolate
adolescents from their families and friends.

In addition to his own pre-Net experience, Staples invokes research studies to support his argument. He refers to "researchers" in his sixth paragraph
and "studies" in his eighth, but cites more specific references in paragraphs
7, 8, and 10.

It might be useful to ask students to compare Staples's argument with Gelernter's (*LBR* p. 344, manual, p. 98).

Our third topic, "Do you think that parents should restrict their children's use of the Internet, or supervise it?" can be used as a writing assignment.

Stanley Fish
Why We Built the Ivory Tower (p. 362)

First, a word about Fish's title, or, more specifically, about the "ivory tower." Probably all native speakers of English have heard the term—though a few may confuse it with the Ivy League. The term is commonly used with a negative connotation, i.e., with the suggestion that the resident of the ivory tower—isolated, detached, withdrawn, perhaps selfish and effete—has very little idea of what is going on in the real world. But Fish uses the term positively. He doesn't say so, but he sees the ivory tower (the college or university) as something like the scientist's laboratory (we wish he had said this), a place where the scientist ardently engages in disinterested study. Far from being detached from reality, the scientist pursues it, puts it under the microscope—but does not use his study as a tool to shape his or her own character, or the character of assistants and students.

Fish here, as in many of his other essays, uses a punchy style:

> [D]o your job; don't try to do someone else's job, as you are unlikely to be qualified; and don't let anyone else do your job. (paragraph 1)

It's hard to see how any instructor can take issue with this statement. But the problem comes when Fish gets around to defining college teacher's job, which he sees as limited to "the search for truth and the dissemination of it through teaching" (paragraph 10).

Most of the essay consists of asserting that the job of a college teacher is *not* "forming character" or "fashioning citizens" or teaching "civic responsibility" (paragraph 7). Probably most teachers of the sciences would agree, though many would add that in (say) their physics course they teach truths about physics but in their other roles as human beings—parent, friend, citizen, etc.— they may hope to form character, fashion citizens, and teach civic responsibility. On the campus these aims may not come out in the classroom, but they may well come out in a teacher's role as an advisor and as a member of committees. Fish does grant that moral issues come up in matters of "plagiarizing and shoddy teaching" (paragraph 9), but he insists that instructors concern themselves only with the moral issues of the academy, not those of democracy.

This assertion is bound to provoke a variety of responses, ranging from "It's about time someone told professors to stick to their job" to "If teaching is nothing more than telling students about the 'truth' I have discovered in my field, I wouldn't be in this business because I don't think I can talk to students three times a week for thirty weeks about the admittedly small truths I think I have discovered, such as the presence (or lack of presence) of an inner stage in the Elizabethan theater, or Shakespeare's use of silence in his history plays, or. . . ."

Fish probably is talking chiefly about acdemicians in institutions where the pressure to publish is very high ("Performing academic work responsibly and at the highest level is a job big enough for any scholar and for any institution" [paragraph 12]), but we have a hunch he would say that *all* teachers at *all* institutions should refrain from trying to form character, partly on the grounds that they are "unlikely to be qualified" (paragraph 1).

A question: Virtually all instructors will agree, we think, that colleges and universities should teach students to think critically, but exactly what is "critical *thinking*"? We take it to mean, among other things, an awareness of one's own assumptions—an awareness that may help to extend one's intellectual horizon, to see merit in views previously dismissed unthinkingly. If we are on the right track here, aren't we pretty much saying that critical thinking—a primary aim in higher education—inevitably has moral and civic as well as intellectual dimensions? Discuss.

Inevitably Fish's essay connects with—because it is so opposed to—Eggers's "Serve or Fail," on requiring students to perform some sort of social service while they are in school.

Wu-tsu Fa-yen
Zen and the Art of Burglary (p. 365)

We include this story for three reasons: (1) we like it; (2) it illustrates methods of teaching, namely, teaching by narrating and by analogy; and (3) its gist is that teaching is not always a matter of stuffing knowledge into a student, for at least some kinds of knowledge are already within the student and need only to be perceived. (We are trying to get at this in our questions in the text; in Zen philosophy, *satori* is not the acquisition of something new but, rather, a perception of something already within us, although usually unperceived because our habit of analytic thought obscures our intuition.)

By the way, although this story, with its emphasis on sudden enlightenment, will probably seem characteristically Zen-like to anyone who knows anything at all about Zen Buddhism, that is only because the Rinzai school (of which Wu-tsu was a member) is the most popular in the United States. But not all Zen Buddhism emphasizes suddenness. The Soto school, for example, practices silent meditation in order to arrive at gradual enlightenment.

Topics for Critical Thinking and Writing

1. Make up a story to illustrate the nature of enlightenment. Or make up a story to illustrate the nature of one of the following: religious faith, patriotism, charity.

2. What relevance does Zen have to secular education? (Or to a sport or skill? Some instructors may want to make use—in the classroom or on the court—of W. Timothy Gallwey's *The Inner Game of Tennis* (1981). This how-to-do-it book includes a few Zen stories and is said to have raised the level of tennis playing.)

Toni Cade Bambara
The Lesson (p. 366)

It would be hard to find a less strident and more delightful story preaching revolution. At its heart "The Lesson" calls attention to the enormous inequity in the distribution of wealth in America, and it suggests that black people ought to start thinking about "what kind of society it is in which some people can spend on a toy what it would cost to feed a family of six or seven" for a year. That the young narrator does not quite get the point of Miss Moore's lesson—and indeed steals Miss Moore's money—is no sign that the lesson has failed. (Presumably Miss Moore doesn't much care about the loss of her money; the money is well lost if it helps the narrator, who plans to spend it, to see the power of money.) In any case, Sugar gets the point, and the narrator has been made sufficiently uneasy ("I sure want to punch somebody in the mouth") so that we sense she will later get the point. The last line of the story seems to refer to her ability to outrun Sugar, but in fact they are going in different directions. Sugar races to spend the money on cake, potato chips, and ice cream sodas; Sylvia, deferring such pleasures, heads for the Drive "to think this day through." There are, then, larger implications in "ain't nobody gonna beat me at nuthin."

Questions 1 and 2 following the text can be answered in an essay of 500 to 1,000 words. See our discussions in this manual for questions inviting comparison of "The Lesson" with "Graduation" (manual, p. 92). Also see the discussion of "The Myth of the Cave" (manual, p. 89).

A Casebook on Testing and Grading

Paul Goodman
A Proposal to Abolish Grading (p. 373)

In discussing this essay students are likely to confirm Goodman's worst fears. They will argue *for* grading because they want to be admitted to veterinary school, or because they need grades on transcripts to apply to a four-year college, or for a job, or because they know they wouldn't work hard in courses without grades. The difficulty in teaching this essay, then, is getting the discussion to focus on the function of grading in education, not in certification; that is, in getting the discussion to focus on the quality of Goodman's argument.

Goodman is not as helpful as he might be. How, for example, do you indicate a student's weaknesses on a test without grading? There are ways, but Goodman doesn't bother to explain them. (For an example of a good explanation, see Paul B. Diederich, *Measuring Growth in English* [1974].)

Topic for Critical Thinking and Writing

Either support or counter Goodman's thesis by drawing on your own experience.

Diane Ravitch
In Defense of Testing (p. 376)

We like Ravitch's opening paragraph—a punchy short sentence followed by two longer sentences that offer concrete details to support the initial broad generalization. Here is the paragraph:

No one wants to be tested. We would all like to get a driver's license without answering questions about right of way or showing that we can parallel park a car. Many future lawyers and doctors probably wish they could join their profession without taking an exam.

Given the title of the essay, "In Defense of Testing," however, we know what is coming: "But tests and standards are a necessary fact of life." So far she hasn't proved anything or, rather, hasn't proved anything other than that she can hold a reader's attention by writing clearly. And that's quite a lot.

In her third and fourth paragraphs she looks at the harm that tests have done. It's always a good strategy to grant that your side of the argument has its weaknesses and the other side has its strengths. But, she argues, we now see clearly that the proper role of tests is not to "ration" education but to "improve" it. Hard to quarrel with her here. The fifth paragraph continues the rosy view ("enormous benefits"), and the sixth tells us what "good tests" should be like. Her final paragraph opens with a sentence that probably engenders assent from almost all readers ("Performance in education means the mastery of both knowledge and skills"), though perhaps a hypersensitive reader sniffs danger: "Performance"—a word used by persons who value credentials too highly; "mastery"—a word that is not only sexist but that has a faint aroma of cruelty. And then the bombshell: "this is why it is reasonable to test teachers to make sure they know their subject matter, as well as how to teach it to young children." Well, we should have seen it coming. Ravitch's title is "In Defense of Testing," so why shouldn't testing refer to teachers as well as to students? Still, her essay is almost entirely directed toward the testing of students, not teachers.

Joy Alonso
Two Cheers for Examinations (p. 378)

We think Alonso does a good job of defending tests, though inevitably she doesn't touch on every possible aspect of the topic.

For instance, she says nothing about take-home examinations, though perhaps we can guess that she might approve provided that they called upon students to review the material for the term and required students to synthesize material, i.e., provided that the take-home examinations were not in effect another research paper or critical paper on a relatively narrow topic. We should mention, too, an obvious problem: it is possible that the responses a student submits for a take-home examination are not entirely his or her own work. In our view there is nothing wrong with students discussing the topics among themselves—we think such discussion is to be encouraged—but there is something very wrong if one student writes the examination for another. One of our colleagues has suggested (we ourselves have not seen this phenomenon) that the problem is not dishonesty but a general leveling down of ideas. In this instructor's view, students who get together and discuss a topic sometimes turn in rather bland papers, papers that reflect something like a synthesis of the group's discussion, rather than a paper with an individual point of view. Possibly another objection to the take-home examination is that some students can have the benefit of group discussion whereas others—notably those who cannot remain on campus for a discussion but must go to a job—are left to their own devices. We think that these objections do add up to something significant, and in most of our courses we prefer not to give take-home examinations.

But the two- or three-hour in-class examination can also be criticized. Why, some students and instructors ask, should students have to race against the clock? The usual reply, and it has some merit, is that in school (as in life) there are all kinds of timetables, schedules, deadlines. Part of the value of an examination is that it asks students to know the material well enough to present it within a certain timeframe. Other kinds of assignments—short essays, book reports, research papers—allow students to work at their own pace (within limits).

Another issue that Alonso does not address is the instructor's difficulty in making up a fair examination. It's always tempting to include yet one more question, but surely it's a mistake to give students more than they can handle in the time they have available. If anything, it's a good idea, we have found, to prepare an exam that students can complete with time left over, so that they can review what they've written and maybe insert a second thought or two and double-check answers they are unsure about.

Still, having pointed out the issues that Alonso does not address, we want to end by saying we think her essay is judicious, and, given the limits of her space, she does a good job. One tiny point, however: in her talk, when she engagingly cited a source for her title, saying that she didn't want to be accused of plagiarism, she apparently assumed that her audience—chiefly teachers of English—would recognize that she was alluding to Forster's *Two Cheers for Democracy*, but first-year students may mistakenly think that Forster wrote something called "Two Cheers for Examinations."

9

WORK AND PLAY

Illustrations

Dorothea Lange
Lettuce Cutters, Salinas Valley (p. 384)

Lange was for some years a successful portrait photographer in California, but during the Depression she turned to taking documentary photographs of migrant workers. Her photographs, taken under the auspices of the Farm Security Administration, were widely reproduced in newspapers and magazines. She is rightly given much of the credit for subsequently improved working conditions.

Lange pasted on the door of her darkroom these words: "The contemplation of things as they are, without error or confusion, without substitution or imposture, is in itself a nobler thing than a whole harvest of invention." (She attributed them to Francis Bacon, and they certainly are Baconian, but to our ear the quotation is somewhat modernized. We will be grateful to anyone who can tell us if Lange has or has not quoted exactly.) "The contemplation of things as they are. . . ." But of course the camera does not really give us "things as they are." It gives us things as they appear at a particular moment, from a particular angle, reproduced on a particular kind of film and paper, and so on. In *Lettuce Cutters* we see things from a low angle, so that the almost uniformly bent figures of indeterminate sex seem like laboring beasts or even four-legged headless monsters ponderously moving along the earth. The earth itself, with its rows of lettuce, looks rather like a great field of mud in which these primitive creatures are quite at home. But the low angle also allows the figures to rise into the sky; if they are rooted in the earth, they are nevertheless creatures of an upper region. The work is brutalizing, but these workers endure. (By the way, these workers are Filipinos. Much of the stoop labor in California has been done by people other than WASPs.)

A note on pictures of workers. Before the nineteenth century, except for Brueghel's peasants and the peasants in medieval pictures of the months or the seasons, there were few important pictures of unskilled workers. Around the middle of the nineteenth century, however, especially after the Revolution of 1848, a new faith in the dignity of labor produced important pictures of workers, for example, Millet's *The Gleaners*. In such pictures, the unskilled worker (especially the rural laborer) is at last treated heroically or at least given the scale and care that previously had been given chiefly to heroic or religious subjects. For a good discussion of this point, see Chapter 3 of Linda Nochlin's *Realism* (1971).

For an exercise using this picture, see suggestion 2 for writing on Auden (manual, p. 115).

Helen Levitt
Children (p. 385)

There are plenty of good pictures of children playing, showing their joy on a swing or their intense concentration while at bat. And surely joy and concentration are proper parts of play. But Helen Levitt's photograph captures a quality of child's play that we have rarely seen in other pictures: not joy or effort but grace. Pictures of children playing delight us more often by the child's charming clumsiness than by grace. Levitt's children, however, by putting on masks, have been able to give themselves new identities, to remove themselves for a moment from the troublesome reality of being (say) Johnny Jones of 31 Spruce Street, son of John and Mary Jones. Now—at least until they take off their masks—they have no nagging parents, no homework assignment, for they are new people; three bits of cloth or paper have permitted the children to enter into a land of heart's desire.

We see the three children in progressive stages of disguise. At the rear, the girl is just putting on her mask, and so she is still a girl putting on a mask. The child in the middle is masked and is moving (somewhat tentatively) onstage. But at the front right we see the completion of the process, a masked child onstage, secure in his mask or new identity, and therefore assuming a marvelously cocky and graceful pose. If the not-yet-masked little girl at the rear, in her dark coat, is almost swallowed up by her environment, the fully masked little boy at the right transforms his environment, turning it into his castle by the way he crosses one leg over the other and puts a confident hand on the railing.

Short Views

Topics for Critical Thinking and Writing

1. "Winning is not the most important thing; it's everything," is heard less often than "Winning isn't everything; it's the only thing," but ours is the earliest published version attributed to Lombardi. Students can be invited to compare the two versions, as well as to compare both with what may be Lombardi's source: Bill Veeck's "I do not think that winning is the most important thing; I think winning is the only thing."

2. Write an essay in which, on the basis of your own knowledge of serious sport, you support or reject Orwell's statement. (Orwell is giving a new twist to the old idea that sport is a sort of training ground for military virtues; cf. the business about Waterloo being won on the playing fields of Eton. For Orwell, sport does indeed resemble war, but in dirtiness rather than in courage, discipline, or any kind of heroism.)

Bertrand Russell
Work (p. 389)

It may come as something of a surprise to notice, on rereading this lucid essay, that Russell does not do much in the way of making us see. He refers to Lenin, Michelangelo, and Shakespeare, but for the most part he does not descend to individuals; rather, he speaks of "most people," "most of the idle rich," "women whose lives are occupied with housework," and so on. One hesitates to mention it in class, but the truth is that one can be clear without offering lots of specific, visual details. And after all, it is not the business of a philosopher to amuse or to animate, but to think clearly and to write clearly. Still, Russell's admirably clear essay would have been a trifle more interesting and perhaps therefore even a trifle more persuasive if it were richer in presenting the particulars of this world—the sort of thing Russell does do when he glances at Michelangelo and Shakespeare. Yet we don't mean to suggest that the essay loses sight of this world. Every reader will respond to such a sentence as "A boy who can stand on his head becomes reluctant to stand on his feet," and every older male reader will respond to "A man who runs three-mile races will cease to find pleasure in this occupation when he passes the age at which he can beat his own previous record."

A word about Russell's organization, which is worth discussing, especially if you are studying the essay as a piece of persuasive writing. At the end of the fourth paragraph Russell announces the structure of the rest of his essay, which will move from work that is "mildly interesting" to work that is "worthy to absorb the whole energies of a great man." Obviously if he began with the last sort of work, most of his readers would feel that he is not talking about them; they would feel that he is elitist. And so he begins with the familiar and then moves to the remote.

Topics for Critical Thinking and Writing

1. Russell gives a few reasons for the unsatisfying nature of housework. In a paragraph or two give some additional reasons.

2. Compare Russell and Auden on work and its relationship to happiness.

W. H. Auden
Work, Labor, and Play (p. 395)

As question 1 in the text suggests, we find Auden's first three paragraphs confusing. In the first paragraph, the first sentence introduces Arendt's distinction between work and labor. The second and third sentences fail to make clear how they elaborate or comment on Arendt's definitions, because the terms being defined—"work" and "labor"—do not appear nor are they clearly referred to. It's only when we get through the third and fourth sentences that we can infer that the word "happy" in the second and third sentences describes the worker, but not the laborer. The second paragraph further confuses us by introducing a new distinction, between "labor" and "play," leaving "work" out entirely. We must wait until the fifth paragraph to have "work" reintroduced—and then all becomes clear.

Why are we willing to tolerate this muddle and to read on? It's not simply because Auden's topic is interesting and because his commonsense tone assures us that he will, soon enough, be making sense. Rather, unlike our students who have been assigned to read "Work, Labor, and Play" in a textbook, we originally encountered the piece browsing through Auden's commonplace book, for pleasure. Picking up *A Certain World*, we didn't expect (or want) sustained discourse, but something akin to the pleasure of good conversation: Auden thinking about what Arendt said and responding to it. If "Work, Labor, and Play" offers students a model of writing, it is a model of a journal entry, not an essay. And the difference in the circumstances and expectations of their reading of the piece and ours might be used as analogous to the differences in attitudes that define work, labor, and play.

Topics for Critical Thinking and Writing

1. Write an essay of approximately 500 words: If you have ever been a worker or a laborer, describe the job and your attitude toward it that determined whether, in Auden's terms, you were a worker or a laborer.

2. With Auden's definitions of work, labor, and play in mind, write a paragraph on Lange's photograph *Lettuce Cutters.*

John Updike
Early Inklings (p. 397)

First, about the title: an "inkling" can mean a hint, here a hint of Updike's future career as a writer. But by chance the word also contains the work "ink," a tool of his craft. Or, as he says in his concluding line, "This was my element, ink on paper."

There are many other amusing touches in this brief narrative: the fly-swatting job at age six, which "did not open out into a career"; the movie theater sending pairs of boys out to "territories as remote as Mohnton and Sinking Spring" (clearly towns neighboring Shillington); the sunglass lenses, "overcooked hemispheres, with their blank and slippery eyes"; and the charming final sentence, echoing the title.

Updike is one of our most elegant stylists, but we like to call attention to his use of ordinary means, available to all, to ensure readability and clarity. We note, for example, in paragraph 1, "My first paying job"; in paragraph 2, "Next . . . I worked for a weekly pass"; in paragraph 3, "Next, a dark chapter"; in paragraph 5, "When I was eighteen. . . ." *Use transitions!*, we say.

Updike was born in 1932, when America was, as he says, "haunted" by the Great Depression. There are only a few references to the Depression in this brief piece: the seven-cent fare for the trolley car that Updike and his partner would save by walking home from neighboring towns, the "malnourished city-dwelling co-workers." President Carter and Updike were near contemporaries (Carter was born in 1924). Some students might want to compare, in a paragraph or two, the glimpse of Updike's life during the Depression with President Carter's (p. 628).

Gloria Steinem
The Importance of Work (p. 399)

Steinem assumes that work is a basic human right, but she argues that women should assert that right, first by giving up the passive defense "womenworkbecausewehaveto" and then by actively supporting policies that guarantee a job for everyone who wants one, regardless of sex or need, however need might be defined.

"Weworkbecausewehaveto" should be abandoned for several reasons. First, it is deceptive. Women work for the same reasons men do: out of economic need and for security, certainly, but also for self-respect, personal fulfillment, the good of society, and pleasure. Second, the passive defense of women working is dangerous. Unless the right to work is firmly established, women will remain vulnerable to discriminatory policies that rob their families and country of the full use of their talents, and they will deny themselves "one of life's basic pleasures."

The argument is clearly addressed to women. It is not only from the consistent use of the first person pronouns "we" and "us" that we infer this but also from the scope and the tone of Steinem's arguments. (After all, she could have been writing about herself and other women for a mixed audience, or for an audience of men.) She does not really argue the point that, regardless of need or the economic climate, women have a basic human right to work, as she might have with an audience of potential competitors or adversaries. Rather, she assumes that her audience not only agrees with her on that score but that they are already committed feminists, part of a movement to whom she offers clarification and direction. (See in particular paragraph 7 beginning "I'm afraid the answer is often no.") Of course, men can be, and many men are, feminists. So we might modify our definition of audience here to include feminists of either sex (as one of Philip Roth's characters, growing up in an immigrant Jewish family in Newark, used the word Catholics, as he said, to include the Protestants).

Steinem supports her argument with authority and style. In addition to reasons and subtle arguments that probe the implications of "facts," she has facts—from statistics about the gross national product and the labor force to the real reason for the high price of steak. And although she clearly looks forward to "the real work revolution" when "all productive work [including child rearing] is rewarded," her argument in these pages is backed by such relatively conservative authorities as the *Wall Street Journal* and the U.S. Congress, whose Economic Act of 1946 she quotes.

She argues vigorously and with apparent relish, jostling figures ("a whopping 69 percent") and joshing received ideas ("good old fashioned penis envy" and "the sons-in-law who sleep their way to power"). But along with colloquial and informal diction, she also employs to good advantage the periodic sentence for weight and emphasis (see the last two sentences in paragraph 18). We note also her use, for emphasis, of one-sentence paragraphs and might look at them in class to clarify when a one-sentence paragraph is useful and when it is not.

Topic for Critical Thinking and Writing

All of the questions following the text can be used for writing exercises. In addition, we suggest the following to our students: Reread paragraph 9, focusing on the second sentence. In your experience, is it true that "a paid job may be preferable to the dole, even when the hand-out is coming from a family member"? Write a paragraph or two on your experience with a "dole" and your reflections on it. (We assume that most students can compare money earned with money received as an allowance, gift, or inheritance and can reflect on their attitudes about money and themselves as a consequence.)

Felice N. Schwartz
The "Mommy Track" Isn't Anti-Woman (p. 404)

As the defensive title hints, Schwartz's proposal can seem (and for some people is) "anti-woman." Probably almost everyone today agrees that a woman should not have to choose between a career and a family, but probably almost everyone today also agrees that—given today's conditions—having children interposes a substantial barrier between a woman and a top job.

Why? Because today, as in the past, and despite all of the talk about men sharing in child-rearing, women are still the people primarily responsible for child-rearing. Some husbands make substantial contributions, and some businesses make substantial efforts to assist (for instance, by providing maternal leave, day care, and in a few cases summer camps for youngsters), but often the contributions of husbands and of businesses are slight.

Schwartz angered some women (and some businessmen, too) by suggesting that women should choose between a fast track (go without children, and aim for the top jobs) and a mommy track (have children, and in exchange for a flexible schedule be satisfied with a middle-level job and middle-level pay). As we understand Schwartz, she says that women do indeed cost businesses more than men (because, for instance, women have a higher dropout rate, thus requiring the businesses to engage in the costly process of training a successor), but businesses need women because "Women comprise half the talent and competence in the country" (paragraph 5). She denies that "companies are looking for excuses to send women home again" (paragraph 5). It has been fairly widely reported in the press, however, that many businessmen are looking for such excuses, especially in recessionary times when top executives are more driven to cut costs.

It's our impression that many women do drop out of the fast track when they have a child and do not reenter it. Schwartz argues that many (most?) women would trade top jobs (and the high pay that goes with them) for jobs that offered less money and demanded less but allowed them a chance to spend time with their families. Businesses would benefit from such an arrangement because they would be retaining talented, trained women in middle-level (lower-paying) jobs. At least three things about Schwartz's essay apparently bother some readers: (1) she seems to accept the idea that mothers should make greater sacrifices than fathers; (2) she seems, despite occasional assertions to the contrary, to assume that businesses won't do much more to recognize family obligations (of fathers as well as of mothers); and (3) her position allows a reader to conclude that a woman makes a firm decision at, say, age 25 about what sort of life she wants to live, whereas in fact (or at least in the eyes of certain readers) women, like men, may change their plans. The critical child-rearing years may occupy only a brief period in a woman's life, and they can occur early or at a later stage. A woman may have children soon after entering the job market, leave, and then a few years later reenter the market and wish to aim for the top, or on the other hand she may have children relatively late. Schwartz's plan, some people say, assumes that a woman can and must decide early.

These are large issues, and they will be debated vigorously in the classroom. We have a question about a small detail in Schwartz's essay, but it may reveal a larger difficulty. The end of her next-to-last paragraph goes like this: Women should not "be penalized for wanting to make a substantial commitment to family. Achievement should not be a function of whether an employee has children. Success is the reward of talent, hard work and commitment."

Her twofold use of "commitment" troubles us. In the first part of the quotation she speaks of "commitment to family," and in the second she speaks of the rewards—presumably including money—that are due to "hard work and commitment." But, again as we understand it, her essay assumes that in general women are less fully committed to the job than men. And it also perhaps assumes that our society won't greatly change in its assignment of child care. Taking a leaf from Schwartz's book, businessmen can presumably say (and this is what has bothered many of her critics), "Yes, we reward commitment—commitment to our business, and we have no room for people who are not committed."

Virginia Woolf
Professions for Women (p. 410)

How can we characterize the tone of the marvelous first paragraph? Ironic? Brisk? Incisive? Witty? Something of a combination of all of these, but if we had to choose one word, perhaps it would be "astringent." The first half of the paragraph is on the whole modest, the gist being encapsulated in "Thus, when I came to write, there were very few material obstacles in my way." The second half of the paragraph is wittier (the joke about being able to buy enough paper to write all of Shakespeare's plays), more self-deprecatory (the joke is continued in "if one has a mind that way"), and more outraged (because society thinks of writing as cheap and harmless, it lets women write). And so the paragraph as a whole shows us a woman who claims little for herself but who nevertheless conveys a sense of outrage—with the utmost courtesy, of course.

Topics for Critical Thinking and Writing

1. Question 2 can provide a topic for an autobiographical essay. Question 3 can be answered in an essay that compares a piece of writing—a poem or a fragment of an autobiography—by a contemporary male writer with one by a contemporary female writer.

2. This essay was originally a talk. What gestures and what tones might Woolf have used at certain points, especially at the beginning and the end?

3. Explain what Woolf means by "the phantom" (in the third paragraph) and by the "rock" (in the fifth paragraph). Why is she more explicit about the phantom than about the rock?

4. A research paper: in her first paragraph Woolf mentions Fanny Burney, Aphra Behn, Harriet Martineau, Jane Austen, and George Eliot. Choose one of these women and see what you can discover (from her own writing or from what others have written about her) about her work, her attitude toward it, and the attitude toward it of others important to her.

Henry Louis Gates Jr.
Delusions of Grandeur (p. 415)

Gates's thesis, of course, is that because very few African Americans can make a living out of sports, African-American youths should be encouraged to think of other kinds of careers. He could have begun bluntly, along these lines, and with the amazing statistic that there are only 1,200 professional black athletes in the United States, but he chose to begin with a little story—often a good way to begin. The setting is the bar of a VFW post—a setting doubtless familiar to many readers of *Sports Illustrated*, where Gates's article was published. And instead of beginning with his amazing statistic, he in effect lets us guess and keeps us in suspense, through the guise of reporting the guesses of others. In short, we find the opening highly effective.

Our last question asks about the appeal of stories of defeat (cf. Shakespeare's *Richard II*, "Let us sit upon the ground, / And tell sad stories of the death of kings"). Ever since Aristotle, people have been trying to explain why tragedy is appealing, and doubtless there are many valid answers, even if there are no definitive answers. (Students might enjoy thinking about the reasons why sad songs, for instance, the blues, are treasured.) If we take pride in the successes of our ancestors, we also take pride in their sufferings (often brought on by their refusal to submit) and even in their failures. King David, for example, one of the most beloved figures in the Hebrew Bible, remains in our memory not only as the youthful hero who killed Goliath, and as the loyal friend who grieved for the death of Jonathan, but also as the fallible man who slept with Bathsheba and who in effect murdered her husband. Indeed, of these three stories of David, many people would say the saddest story is the most moving. If your class includes students from a range of cultures, you will probably hear some stories of the fall of heroes—for instance, the Jews at Masada, or Cuchulain of Ireland, or the kamikaze pilots of Japan.

Sir Thomas More
Work and Play in Utopia (p. 418)

It is probably fair to say that More's *Utopia* is both a serious and a playful exercise on the topic: what is humanity's highest good, and, since people are imperfect and self-interested, what sort of commonwealth is needed to bring about this highest good? As we will indicate below, it seems that in *Utopia* More assumes the highest good is rational pleasure, but it is impossible to know exactly how serious he was in the book. Certain parts are clearly playful (to show their contempt for wealth, Utopians use chamber pots made of gold and silver, and they fetter prisoners in gold and silver chains), but it is clear that More believes that human unhappiness is rooted in pride, and therefore Utopia has laws that seek to prevent people from becoming proud. Thus all Utopians wear the same garb; no one can lord it over others by wearing designer jeans. Similarly, all Utopians (except scholars) must work at agriculture; no one (again with the exception of scholars) is above manual labor. But for More, universal compulsory labor, in addition to humbling people, reduces the number of hours that each person must work, for if everyone works, the needs of all are supplied by a relatively short work week. (In the England of More's day, the poor worked from dawn to dusk, with a little time off for meals.) The consequence is, as More makes clear at the end of the first excerpt, that all the citizens of Utopia can "devote themselves to the freedom and culture of the mind. For that, they think, is the real happiness of life."

A government that exists to ensure that its citizens live lives of rational pleasure (rather than a government that exists to let each citizen engage in the pursuit of whatever sort of happiness he or she desires) may well strike modern readers as totalitarian. Still, one can argue that every government is in some degree repressive (it conscripts citizens, it prohibits certain acts, it imposes compulsory education, it takes some of our income). More would perhaps claim that a Utopian is free to pursue pleasure up to the point where it conflicts with duty to society. Whether or not a citizen of the United States is similarly restricted may be the subject of lively class discussion.

Justice Brandeis in 1928 (*Olmstead v. United States*) asserted that "the makers of our Constitution undertook to secure conditions favorable to the pursuit of happiness. . . . They conferred, as against the Government, the right to be let alone—the most comprehensive of rights and the right most valued by civilized men." But in fact Americans are not free to indulge in every sort of pleasure or even in every sort that does not obviously harm other people.

Minors cannot buy liquor or pornography, and motorcyclists can't have the fun of riding without helmets. Bull fighting, cock fighting, and dog fighting are outlawed, although boxing—the only human sport in which the goal is to incapacitate the opponent—is not. (Advocates of boxing point out that horse racing, parachuting, hang gliding, mountaineering, scuba diving, motorcycling, and college football all have higher mortality rates.)

And there remain the vexing problems of topless bars and pornographic books and films. Macaulay sneered that the Puritans outlawed bear-baiting not so much because it gave pain to the bear as because it gave pleasure to the spectators—but can't one argue that indeed we should not be permitted certain sorts of pleasures? Probably executions are no longer public not so much because we wish to protect the victim's right to privacy as because we feel that spectators should not be allowed to enjoy the spectacle.

In *Utopia and the Ideal Society* (1985), J. C. Davis suggests that Utopias, as opposed to Arcadias or Lands of Cockaygne, (1) assume human beings have their present nature (e.g., Utopias recognize impulses toward aggression); (2) are chiefly concerned with controlling the unpleasant consequences of human nature rather than with the happiness of individuals; and (3) assume that the best method of control is totalitarian discipline (i.e., a powerful legal system). These points seem to us to apply to More's *Utopia*. We take it that although More's emphasis is on pleasure, he assumes that only certain kinds of pleasures are sound or acceptable and that pride is at the root not only of unacceptable pleasures but of most of the evil in the world. Hence (as we have already suggested) More's emphasis on nearly universal compulsory manual labor and on the uniformity of dress.

For commentaries (along with a translation of the entire work) see the Norton edition by Robert M. Adams. Edward Surtz, who is the author of two important books on *Utopia*, has also done an edition with a useful introduction.

Topic for Critical Thinking and Writing

Among the activities that More regards as false pleasures are hunting and gambling. He gives an extended reason for his opposition to hunting, but none for his opposition to gambling; he simply asserts that gambling doesn't give pleasure. Write an essay of 500–750 words on the pleasures that hunting or gambling affords. Note that you need not approve of either activity; you need only try to understand the nature of the pleasure that hunters or gamblers experience.

Black Elk
War Games (p. 424)

Neither this selection from *Black Elk Speaks* nor our other selection from Black Elk, "High Horse's Courting" (p. 180), clearly represents Black Elk's intention in telling his life story to John G. Neihardt. Black Elk's purpose in recalling the past and in selecting Neihardt (who was collecting materials for an epic poem about the West) as his biographer was, in his own words, to preserve "a mighty vision given to a man too weak to use it." But readers of "War Games" may be interested to learn that when Black Elk was four or five, mysterious voices came to him when he was playing, and he later believed that the voices anticipated the first of his power-visions, which occurred when he was nine. The fear he candidly reveals in these pages is a recurring motif in his narrative and is closely related, one feels, to his vocation and to his sense of inadequacy to it. An excellent introduction to *Black Elk Speaks* may be found in Robert Sayre's "Vision and Experience in *Black Elk Speaks,*" *College English* 32 (February 1971).

Topic for Critical Thinking and Writing

Question 2 following "War Games" suggests two ways of writing a description.

Marie Winn
The End of Play (p. 426)

Winn's chief point is that today's children do not engage in "the old kinds of imaginative, traditional 'children's play.'" One of her chief methods of supporting her thesis is to summarize or to quote persons whom she has interviewed ("Psychiatrists have observed . . ."; "A kindergarten teacher confirms . . ."). The method can make for effective persuasive writing, but obviously much depends on the sample interviewed and on the quotations Winn selects from the interview. Probably it is a technique that students should be warned against taking too seriously.

Among the lost kinds of play that Winn mentions are "jump-rope play [and] ball-bouncing play." These forms can be "imaginative" (if, for example, accompanied by fanciful rhymes), but Winn sometimes seems to muddle various kinds of play, and she laments the diminution of all old forms. Moreover, in her emphasis on TV as the villain, she neglects to notice that such relatively new forms of play as skateboard riding and break-dancing are pretty close to the old forms whose demise she laments. If today parents complain that kids "don't ride bicycles as much as we used to," perhaps their great-great-great-grandparents complained that the invention of the bicycle was a curse, because kids "don't walk and run as much as we used to."

Another point: in her next-to-last paragraph, Winn asks, "What then are these so-called children to do for fulfillment if their desire to play has been vitiated and yet their entry into the working world of adulthood must be delayed for many years?" Winn assumes that she has adequately demonstrated that the desire for play has been vitiated, but one may wonder if this is so. One may wonder, too, if the newer forms of play (e.g., video games) do not allow students to indulge in what can be called pure play and at the same time nevertheless help to prepare many children for the newer forms of adult jobs. If so, play and work still are related as they were related in the earlier societies that Winn talks about in paragraph 22.

By the way, Winn's assumption that television has reduced play (an assumption that was the basis of her previous book, *The Plug-in Drug* [1977]) is not universally shared. Various essayists in *Children and Television* (1976), edited by Ray Brown, offer evidence suggesting that although watching television reduces time spent in going to movies and in reading comic books, it does not reduce time spent on hobbies, organized sports, or playing musical instruments.

Winn's essay can easily be related to other essays in this section of the text. For an example of play in a preindustrial society, see Black Elk, "War Games," in this chapter.

Topics for Critical Thinking and Writing

1. List the causes Winn cites for the decline of play, and evaluate her argument concerning one of them.

2. Analyze Winn's methods of argument. What devices does she use to persuade her readers?

3. Drawing on your own experience, write an essay supporting or rejecting Winn's contention that you were deprived of the sort of play that she extols. You may want to narrow the topic, comparing only your kindergarten experiences with Winn's remarks on kindergarten.

4. If you have enjoyed playing video games or watching TV—even perhaps only one program—respond to Winn in about 500 words, trying to convey the pleasure (and perhaps the value) of this activity.

5. Winn argues that video games are "adult-created mechanisms" and thus are "less likely to impart a sense of mastery and fulfillment." Can the same thing be said of a book written for children? If when you were a child you read books, explain to Winn why you found it pleasurable to do so.

James Paul Gee
From Video Games, Learning about Learning (p. 433)

Gee devotes the first half of his essay, eight paragraphs, to his experience with video games, first an account of playing them with his small son, and then alone, playing adult games. He reveals, along the way, that he is a "baby-boomer," and that although his profession was, formerly, as a theoretical linguist, he is now "in education." These biographical details help to establish his credentials as he offers a critique of video games, particularly of their merits.

His argument begins with three "revelations": that video games are "profoundly difficult," that playing them was "a life-enhancing experience," and that, despite their length and difficulty, they are extremely successful—they sell millions of copies. These revelations lead him to conclude that successful video games incorporate good principles of learning and that the theory of learning in good video games is close to the "best theories of learning in cognitive science." (We confess that we do not follow his argument here and we wish that he had devoted a paragraph or two explaining both what he means by "principles of learning" and the similarities between those principles in cognitive science and in video games.)

He further concludes that the theory of learning in good video games is similar to that of the best science instruction in schools, but that good science instruction is becoming rare, and that other instruction in schools commonly fails to measure up to the design of good video games.

Since most students have had more experience with video games than most instructors, class discussion of Gee's article should prove lively and fruitful. A good option is to ask for a student volunteer to lead the discussion. When that leader runs out of steam, a second and then a third can take over.

James C. McKinley Jr.
It Isn't Just a Game: Clues to Avid Rooting (p. 436)

Why, according to McKinley, do people become sports fans? He fields a number of possibilities. Identification with a team gives fans a sense of community that might once have been offered by religion, politics, or family but is now absent or lacking in the fan's life; sports may thus fill a void. Fans might be reacting as their early ancestors reacted, treating sports heroes as if they were warriors representing and protecting the tribe. Fans may hope to attain respect by their connection with athletes, "basking in reflected glory." Attending a sports event may yield a catharsis, a release; the fan "gives free rein to his anger or gloats openly in triumph" (paragraph 34). The fan's commitment to a team may cost him or her friendships, but through the commitment the fan makes new friends who share it.

Is rooting for a team good or bad for one's health? According to McKinley, recent studies have found that "deep attachment to a team can be healthy" (paragraph 47). "[A]n intense interest in a team can buffer people from depression and foster feelings of self-worth and belonging" (paragraph 47). Of course, this view fails to accord with studies that link the ardor of sports fans and their aggressive behavior. Or does it? Perhaps beating his wife makes the fan feel good, relieves his depression—it's simply not good for the wife's health!

"It Isn't Just a Game: Clues to Avid Rooting" does not pretend to be a scholarly study; it is a newspaper report, and we expect that many students will enjoy reading it and arguing about its premises and conclusions.

John Updike
A & P (p. 442)

It may be useful for students to characterize the narrator and see if occasionally Updike slips. Is "crescents," in the fourth sentence, too apt a word for a speaker who a moment later says, "she gives me a little snort," and "if she'd been born at the right time they would have burned her over in Salem"? If this is a slip, it is more than compensated for by the numerous expressions that are just right.

"A & P" is a first-person story, and in its way is about growing up. Invite students to characterize the narrator as precisely as possible. Many will notice his hope that the girls will observe his heroic pose, and some will notice, too, his admission that he doesn't want to hurt his parents. His belief (echoing Lengel's) that he will "feel this for the rest of his life" is also adolescent. But his assertion of the girls' innocence is attractive and brave.

Some readers have wondered why Sammy quits. Nothing in the story suggests that he is a political rebel, or that he is a troubled adolescent who uses the episode in the A & P as a cover for some sort of adolescent emotional problem. An extremely odd article in *Studies in Short Fiction*, 23 (1986): 321–23, which seeks to connect Updike's story with Hawthorne's "Young Goodman Brown," says that "Sammy's sudden quitting is not only a way of attracting the girls' attention but also a way of punishing himself for lustful thoughts." Surely this is nonsense, even further off the mark than the same author's assertion that Queenie's pink bathing suit "suggests the emerging desires competing with chastity" (322). Sammy quits because he wants to make a gesture on behalf of these pretty girls, who in appearance and in spirit (when challenged, they assert themselves) are superior to the "sheep" and to the tedious Lengel. Of course Sammy hopes his gesture will be noticed, but in any case the gesture is sincere.

What sort of fellow is Sammy? Is he a male chauvinist pig? An idealist? A self-satisfied deluded adolescent? Someone who thinks he is knowledgeable but who is too quick to judge some people as sheep? Maybe all of the above, in varying degrees. Certainly his remark that the mind of a girl is "a little buzz like a bee in a glass jar" is outrageous—but later he empathizes with the girls, seeing them not as mindless and not as mere sex objects but as human beings who are being bullied. If we smile a bit at his self-dramatization ("I felt how hard the world was going to be to me hereafter"), we nevertheless find him endowed with a sensitivity that is noticeably absent in Lengel.

Helpful studies of Updike include: George W. Hunt, *John Updike and the Three Great Secret Things: Sex, Religion, and Art* (1980); *Critical Essays on John Updike*, ed. William R. McNaughton (1982); Donald J. Greiner, *John Updike's Novels* (1984); and Julie Newman, *John Updike* (1988).

Students will likely be familiar with Updike's name; some will have seen the film version of his novel, *The Witches of Eastwick* (1984). But because he has written so much, students may be unsure what by Updike they should read. For starters, we recommend the early novel, *Rabbit, Run* (1960), and the short story collections, *Pigeon Feathers* (1962) and *Problems* (1979). Updike is also an extraordinarily versatile and accomplished literary critic. His essays and reviews have been collected in *Hugging the Shore: Essays and Criticism* (1983); *Odd Jobs: Essays and Criticism* (1991); and *More Matter: Essays and Criticism* (1999).

W. H. Auden
The Unknown Citizen (p. 448)

In "The Unknown Citizen" the speaker's voice is obviously not the poet's. The speaker—appropriately unidentified in a poem about a society without individuals—is apparently a bureaucrat. For such a person, a "saint" is not one who is committed to spiritual values but one who causes no trouble.

Topics for Critical Thinking and Writing

1. What is Auden satirizing in "The Unknown Citizen"? (Students might be cautioned to spend some time thinking about whether Auden is satirizing the speaker, the citizen, conformism, totalitarianism, technology, or what.)

2. Write a prose eulogy of 250 words satirizing contemporary conformity or, if you prefer, contemporary individualism.

3. Was he free? Was he happy? Explain.

4. In a paragraph or two, sketch the values of the speaker of the poem, and then sum them up in a sentence or two. Finally, in as much space as you feel you need, judge these values.

10

MESSAGES

Illustrations

Jill Posener
Born Kicking, Graffiti on Billboard, London (p. 452)

Posters of this sort, emphasizing aspects of the female body, present women chiefly as heterosexually desirable physical objects. (In this poster the woman is also infantilized; she is presented as newly hatched and sexually attractive.) Some feminists have countered the messages of advertisers by adding messages of their own that help the viewer to see that the original message is not so innocent as it seems. (Here the use of pairs of the symbol for "female" suggests that probably a lesbian feminist sprayed the counter-message.) Where the advertiser emphasizes the softness and smoothness of the legs, i.e., their sexual attractiveness, the graffiti writer sees the legs as healthily aggressive and converts the legs into an image more acceptable to feminists: "Born Kicking."

Query: Some images of female nudity—for instance, in *Playboy*, and, for that matter, in paintings by the Old Masters—are clearly aimed chiefly at male viewers. But images of female nudity in today's advertisements are aimed chiefly at female viewers. Why are advertisements showing nude or semi-nude women attractive to women? The commonest answer to this question that we have encountered in print is that some female viewers narcissistically identify themselves with the female image depicted. Another answer occasionally given in print is that many women, socialized by a patriarchal culture, negate their own experience and identify with the heterosexual masculine voyeuristic gaze.

Suggested writing assignment: Ask the class to analyze an advertisement that, upon scrutiny, can reasonably be called offensively sexist. What is the ad's overt message? What is its implied message? (Instruct the students to hand in a photocopy of the ad with their analysis.)

Anonymous
Sapolio (p. 453)

First a few words about advertising. Most ads like this one for Sapolio (Latin *sapo* = soap + *oleum* = olive [oil]) try to persuade the viewer, usually with pictures of shaggy dogs, cute children, virile men, or respectable women. (Well, sometimes women are meant to be tastefully disreputable, but that's another story.) They seek to persuade us that by buying the product we shall become happier. This ad is really about Sapolio, of course, but it claims to be about the pleasure—even the sense of rejuvenation—that a sunny spring day affords with a little help from Sapolio. All this happiness will be ours if we buy the product.

Like much commercial art before the mid-1950s, this ad draws heavily on high art. (With the emergence of pop art in the 1950s, the traffic changed direction; high art began to draw heavily on commercial art. See, for example, Richard Hamilton's picture in *LBR*, p. 583). This derivative sort of commercial art thus flattered the viewers, appealing to their elevated appreciation of "art." Most obviously *Sapolio* (from about 1900) shows, in the tendrils that border the picture and that support it in the lower corners, the combined influence of art nouveau and the nineteenth-century arts and crafts movement that was especially associated with William Morris. There is an arty influence, too, in the motif of a person looking through a window, a motif that has its roots in the Renaissance idea that a picture offers not a decoration on a flat surface but, rather, an illusion; one looks through the picture frame as one looks through a window. A common subject is an interior with a window, so that the artist can show skill at depicting not only near and far, indoor and outdoor light, but also the play of sunlight on metal and glass vessels and on polished wood within the room. In pictures by Vermeer, for example, we strongly sense that we are looking through a window into a room, a room that often has yet another window. And in pictures by the Impressionists (especially Monet) and the Post-Impressionists we often sense that we are within a room, looking out and down toward a garden or street scene. Van Gogh, for example, painted many garden scenes from above. The garden depicted in the Sapolio ad, by the way, strongly resembles one of van Gogh's paintings of a garden, a painting which itself is indebted to a Japanese picture of a garden viewed from above. (It may be relevant to mention here that the coming of abstract art, and later of pop art and op art, shuttered the window by insisting that the canvas is a plane that supports not an illusionistic three-dimensional view but a two-dimensional esthetic pattern.)

There is yet more to the sources of the Sapolio ad. The woman-at-the-window is an especially popular motif. One thinks not only of any number of paintings of the Annunciation (in which light streams in on the Virgin) and of such great genre paintings as Vermeer's *Woman Pouring Milk* and his *Young Woman with a Water Jug*, but also of the more immediate sources, nineteenth-century pictures such as John Everett Millais's *Mariana* (1851; reproduced in Timothy Hilton, *The Pre-Raphaelites* [1970], p. 64) and even of William Holman Hunt's *The Awakening Conscience* (1852; in Hilton's book, p. 91). Hunt's picture is a complicated variation, for the woman is a fallen woman who, perceiving from a window the beauty of the garden in springtime (we see the window and the garden reflected in a mirror behind her), leaps from her lover's lap, her face transformed with new morality and therefore new life. The Sapolio lady is of course not fallen, but she (like her kitchenware) is renewed by the sight of the sunny spring.

There is a faintly erotic note in this picture of a new life. It is much fainter, for example, than in Millais's *Mariana,* where the lady's languid posture is almost provocative, or than in pictures of Zeus, as a shower of gold, streaming in upon Danae imprisoned in a tower (the result was that she bore Zeus a son, Perseus), but the erotic note is here nevertheless, in her receptivity to the diagonals that strike her and especially in the cupidlike fertility figures that sport among the growing vegetation at the bottom of the picture.

To point out the rich heritage of this poor picture is not, of course, to say that the picture gets better; it is only to say that even poor pictures owe as much to earlier pictures as they do to life. (We say "even poor pictures," because we assume that the great artists are highly aware of, and usually proud of, their plundering of their predecessors.) But our talk about the artistic traditions behind *Sapolio* has kept us from discussing what to modern viewers may be the most important thing about the picture: it suggests that a woman's greatest pleasure is to have shiny pots, presumably in order to please her husband. Sun and Sapolio are the indispensables that will make her indispensable to a man.

A note about the date of this advertisement. It was run at least as late as 1909, but by then the Sapolio lady was decidedly old-fashioned. Anne Hollander generously responded to our request for information about the date. She wrote:

> I think the date of the original picture in the ad must be 1899, judging from the high collar with flare and the "Flash Gordon" shoulders, and the hair, which is high in front and soft at the back of the neck. After 1903 to around 1906 the hair is even higher in front and bares the back of the neck. Still later, hair softens again (1908–10) but spreads laterally, and collars are worn lower. She's a young woman, not a middle-aged matron in conservative dress.

Topics for Critical Thinking and Writing

1. In 500 words comment on the implicit attitude toward women, or toward the relationship between men and women, in a current advertisement. Hand in a copy of the ad with your essay.

2. In 500 words analyze the appeals (for example, to our possessiveness, frugality, insecurity, desire for pleasure) of an advertisement in a current magazine. Hand in a photocopy of the ad with your essay.

3. Compare *Sapolio* with Joanne Leonard's *Sonia,* also in *LBR,* p. 136.

Short Views

Topics for Critical Thinking and Writing

1. Evaluate Voltaire's remark.

2. Explain Marianne Moore's remark, perhaps clarifying it by giving examples of statements that display "natural reticence."

3. Reread Gary Snyder's comment, and then find a comparable phrase in an advertisement and explain the connection between the words and the advertised product.

Abraham Lincoln
Address at the Dedication of the Gettysburg National Cemetery (p. 456)

Lincoln delivered this "Address" on November 19, 1863, at the site where four months earlier 179,000 Americans had fought. There were 51,000 casualties in the battle.

One reason that the "Address" is brief is that, as Richard A. Lanham points out in *Revising Prose* (1979), the brevity is expressive. "Lincoln took for his subject the inevitable gap between words and deeds. At Gettysburg, this gap was enormous, and the shortness of Lincoln's speech symbolizes just this gap. . . . Lincoln's brevity did not remove the emotion of the occasion but intensified it" (p. 108).

An instructor can profitably go through the address, sentence by sentence, helping students to see that although it seeks by praise to arouse the audience's respect for the dead, it also seeks to move the audience to action. It begins by speaking of an action even earlier than the battle (the bringing to birth of a new nation); it then turns to the present ("Now we are engaged"), and it ends by calling upon the hearers to resolve that the dead did not die in vain, that is, it calls upon the hearers to act so that the nation "shall have a new birth of freedom." The structure is thus past, present, future. The "Address" is at least as much about future deeds of "us the living" as it is about the past deeds of "these honored dead." The praiseworthy deeds of our forefathers and of our dead contemporaries are to be a stimulus to our own future deeds. This emphasis on the future is, of course, related to the praise of the past through the imagery (as Gilbert Highet points out in the next essay) of birth: "conceived in Liberty," "a new birth of freedom."

Gary Willis, in his *Prologue to Inventing America* (1978), pushes the imagery rather far: "The suggested image is . . . a marriage of male heaven ('Our fathers') and female earth ('this continent'). And it is a miraculous conception, a virgin birth. The nation is conceived by a mental act, in the spirit of liberty, and dedicated (as Jesus was in the temple) to a proposition." Maybe. A bit more conservatively one can suggest that the biblical echo of "Four score and seven" (cf. "the days of our years are three score and ten") is picked up in "our fathers" (cf. the beginning of the Lord's Prayer) and perhaps in "brought forth" (cf. "and she brought forth a babe").

Another way of putting the matter is to say that Lincoln delicately enlarges his hearers' understanding of the event. His second paragraph tells them why they are at Gettysburg, and it concludes by affirming that "It is altogether fitting and proper" that they gather for their avowed purpose. The next paragraph, however, courteously diminishes this purpose ("But, in a larger sense, we cannot dedicate . . ."), and it substitutes a grander purpose or obligation.

Philip B. Kunhardt Jr., in an appendix to his *A New Birth of Freedom* (1983), prints the seven early texts of the speech. Two are drafts that Lincoln wrote before he gave the address, two are contemporary reports, and three are versions that Lincoln wrote in the months following his delivery of the speech. Thus, the two drafts say, "We are come to dedicate a portion of it"; and the three later autographs say, "We have come to dedicate a portion of this field." All of the variations are slight, and the wording in modern texts represents a consensus. It is not known exactly what Lincoln actually said at Gettysburg.

Gilbert Highet
The Gettysburg Address (p. 457)

It is useful in class to analyze Highet's rhetorical patterns, in the light of his analysis of Lincoln's. Students can be asked to comment on such passages as "our troubled, adventurous, and valiant past," "[i]nadequately prepared and at first scarcely realized," and the final sentence of the essay.

About question 4 (which is really about Lincoln rather than Highet), Ralph Ross suggests, in *The Art of Reading*, that the passage should not be read as though there were a comma after "government"; "of," he says, should not be emphasized. Ross says it should be read as "government of the people [pause] by the people [pause] for the people." Thus, "it is government over the people. 'Government of the people' is the same as 'the governing of the people.'"

Topics for Critical Thinking and Writing

Highet's essay can provide topics for essays requiring some research. Students might be asked to look up Edward Everett's speech at Gettysburg, to summarize it, analyze it, and compare it with Lincoln's. In his sixth paragraph Highet says, "There are many accounts of the day itself, 19 November 1863." Students might be asked to read some accounts including descriptions of Lincoln, or of the rest of the ceremony, or reactions to the speeches, and to write a paper on their findings. Later in the essay Highet refers to the textbooks Lincoln used as a boy, "full of difficult exercises and skillful devices in formal rhetoric." If any of those texts are available, or if substantial excerpts from them are available in secondary sources, some students might enjoy reading and writing about them.

Robin Lakoff
You Are What You Say (p. 463)

Although Lakoff seems to us to overstate her case in her first three paragraphs ("ridiculed," "damned," "communicative cripples"), her essay, beginning with her fourth paragraph, is informative about language and interesting, if not ground-breaking. Now that she has pointed it out, we think that women probably do use a greater variety of color words than most men do, although we're not entirely sure why. Neither apparently is Lakoff. She says first that women are "encouraged and allowed to make far more precise discriminations in naming colors than men do," but two sentences later this reason is dropped in favor of one more damaging to women: men have the "interesting affairs of the world" to think about, so color distinctions don't interest them. We might ask students for their surmises as to why women use more or different color words than men do. The influence of fashion designers or copywriters may be cited as one reason. A man buying clothes can choose to have his shirts or pajamas or raincoat in tan or blue; a woman is more likely to be asked to choose from among such colors as ecru, mauve, jade, taupe, and sea mist. But she hasn't chosen these words. It is a designer or copywriter, very likely a male, who has chosen them for her. If, however, women talk about fashions in clothes or home furnishings more than men do (and they do), why do they? A man who is a painter, a paint manufacturer, a gardener, or a fabric consultant probably has as many terms for tan or blue as an Eskimo for snow. It's his business to make color discriminations. In what sense is it women's business to know color shades currently in fashion? And why is it their business?

We think students will agree with Lakoff's observation that women do use more tag questions, but exactly why do they use them? Lakoff suggests it is because women lack confidence. But another way of looking at these tag questions is to see them in the context of the fact that in conversations women ask more questions than men do. They do so, one argument holds, because women are more concerned than men with keeping the conversation going. That is, women are busy establishing relationships, whereas men are just conducting business. If the man is unresponsive to a question, the woman tries another question in order to get the brute involved.

About question 3, on which sex talks more and which sex tends to interrupt the other, among the relevant studies are Cheris Kramarae, *Women and*

Men Speaking (1981), and Lionel Tiger, *Women in the Kibbutz* (1975). Tiger points out, for instance, that although the kibbutzim were supposed to promote sexual egalitarianism, at town meetings men did three-quarters of the talking. And somewhere we read (but we can't recall where) that when a man and a woman converse, the man makes 96 percent of the interruptions.

As for question 5, the essay is obviously not merely expository but also polemical. It ends with a call for revolution ("In more ways than one, it's time to speak up"), but even from the start we hear the voice of the rebel. The first two paragraphs, for instance, suggest, by such expressions as "communicative cripples," "the language we were allowed to speak," and "we are ridiculed," that women are enslaved.

Barbara Lawrence
Four-Letter Words Can Hurt You (p. 469)

The first half of Lawrence's essay leans heavily on the etymology of "the best known of the tabooed sexual verbs." This etymology will come as a surprise to students, who may reply that even though they use this obscenity, they can scarcely be accused of sexism since they didn't know the early sadistic implications of the word. But one need not know anything about etymology to know that such words as "screw" and "bang" connote mutilation or violence and contempt. Still, this part of her essay is relatively weak as argument, though it is interesting as exposition. Lawrence probably does well to give this material early (it is informative and it establishes her authority) and to get on to stronger arguments. All of which is to say that some classroom discussion can profitably be spent on Lawrence's organization, as well as on her use of nonlogical persuasive devices such as analogy and irony.

Topic for Critical Thinking and Writing

Lawrence's last sentence implies that our literature and entertainment rely heavily on sexual pejoratives. What evidence (books, films, television programs, magazines) supports her view? Would you defend the use of sexual pejoratives in any of the examples you offer?

Edward T. Hall
Proxemics in the Arab World (p. 471)

A word about the term "behavioral sink," mentioned in question 2. The term apparently comes from ethology (the study of how animals behave in their environment), where it denotes a place of overcrowding in which interaction degenerates. Overcrowded male rats may bite off the tails of their fellows, for example, and overcrowded female rats may neglect their young;

there is an increase in miscarriages; unstable cliques develop and aggression increases. A behavioral sink usually produces a high mortality rate. Consult J. B. A. Calhoun, "A 'Behavioral Sink,'" in E. L. Bliss, ed., *Roots of Behavior* (1968).

Topics for Critical Thinking and Writing

1. Question 4 following the text can be used for a writing assignment.

2. In his next-to-last paragraph Hall says (somewhat unclearly) of the people who live in Arab lands: "Their hierarchy of loyalties is: first to one's self, then to kinsman, townsman, or tribesman, coreligionist and/or countryman." List and explain your own hierarchy of loyalties, or that of a group or community you know well.

3. Hall says (paragraph 4), "I moved my body in such a way as to communicate annoyance." Observe the ways three or four people (including yourself, if you can) express an emotion or several distinct emotions by the ways they move their bodies. Describe the movements accurately and explain what emotions they express.

Deborah Tannen
The Workings of Conversational Style (p. 479)

In our experience, most students are instructed in high school not to use the second person in writing. We like to use Tannen's opening paragraph to discuss this rule (or nonrule). The point is that using the second person engages the reader directly, as if in personal conversation with the author. It is very informal and therefore has limited uses, but it is not incorrect. Another point to make is that in analyzing the tone of the opening paragraph, we are engaging in the kind of linguistic analysis Tannen is about to explain.

Our fifth question may need some explaining. It is our sense that in talking about Americans and what they value (in paragraphs 11 and 12), Tannen almost limits the definition of "American" to white males of Western European extraction. ("Almost" because her writing is a bit vague here, as perhaps it must be if you are going to anthropomorphize an entire multicultural nation: "America as a nation has glorified individuality, especially for men." What can this mean? Does it or does it not glorify individuality for women?)

Our sixth question calls attention to Tannen's assumption in paragraph 16 that women not only talk more to each other than men do but also that their talk to each other is less substantive.

Topics for Critical Thinking and Writing

1. Borrow or rent a videotape of a movie you have enjoyed. Study one scene carefully, taking notes on a short stretch of dialogue between two characters. Then write a linguistic analysis of the messages and metamessages you have observed.

2. Would you like to read more by Tannen? In one typed page, explain your response to both her subject and her style.

Steven Pinker
The Game of the Name (p. 491)

We don't think that anything in Pinker's essay requires any comment from us, except perhaps the reference to Oriental in his final paragraph. Experience has indicated to us that many people do not yet know that this word is out of favor with some. The reason it is out of favor is that it comes from the Latin *oriens* = rising, rising sun, east, from *oriri* = to rise. But of course China, Japan, Korea, and nearby countries are "east" only from a Eurocentric point of view. From the point of view of, say, a Chinese man, there is nothing especially "east" or "eastern" about him, and the sun does not rise in his country; it rises elsewhere, to the east. Similarly, such terms as Middle East and Far East originate in a European point of view.

It's our impression that *orient* and *oriental* are still current in ordinary speech, but many universities have changed the name of what used to be the Department of Oriental Languages to the Department of Asian Languages.

As soon as we wrote the preceding sentence, we were driven by curiosity to look up the etymology of Asia. Zounds! According to the *American Heritage Dictionary* it is "Latin, from Greek, 'region of the rising sun,' from Akkadian *asu*, to go out, (of the sun) to set, akin to Hebrew *yatza*, went out." In short, *Asia* and *Asian* bring us right back to the ousted *oriens*, with its Eurocentric view, only no one seems to know it—yet.

James B. Twitchell
The Marlboro Man: The Perfect Campaign (p. 494)

Does Twitchell prove his claim that the perfect advertising campaign was Marlboro's? In our opinion, he does. His first paragraph informs us that although Marlboro sold poorly in the 1950s, today, "Every fourth cigarette smoked is a Marlboro," and he concludes the paragraph by labeling Leo Burnett's campaign "brilliant," and Marlboro "the most valuable brand in the world." In his sixth paragraph, he analyzes Marlboro's 1950s ad, and in paragraph 10 he compares Philip Morris's advertising of Marlboro with the Camel ad ("I'd Walk a Mile for a Camel") to Marlboro's distinct advantage. (Of the Camel ad: "That he seemingly forgot the spare tire is as stupid as his choosing to smoke.") Twitchell amusingly recounts Marlboro's transformation or "regendering" from the sissy smoke for the Marlboro woman (which did not sell well) to the cowboy smoke which succeeded it. He analyzes the design of the package (paragraph 21) and the Marlboro Man's tattoo (paragraphs 23–26) and explains the success of "Gear Without Limits," the selling of "logo'd stuff to smokers" to counter the feds' ban of cigarette advertising first on TV and now in print (see paragraph 31). In short, his essay fully persuades us that the Marlboro cowboy "is imbedded . . . not just in American culture but in world culture" (paragraph 33).

What devices does Twitchell use to persuade? To begin with, his essay is deeply researched. We don't question for a moment that he knows what he is writing about, and he provides us with a list of works cited. Second, his essay is successfully organized. His paragraphs move us steadily forward from the early 1950s to the 1990s. And, in addition to Twitchell's scholarship and the tight structuring of his argument, his prose is lively, often amusing. "Let's face it, the Camel man was downright stupid. . . . A camel seems intelligent in comparison" (paragraph 10). The Marlboro cowboy Leo Burnett had in mind was "A slightly roughed up, *High Noon* Gary Cooper, a lite-spaghetti Clint Eastwood" (paragraph 17). "With this package you are the decorated conqueror. You burn bridges, bust broncos, confront stuff like lung cancer" (paragraph 21).

We want students to notice the variety of Twitchell's sentences. In the first paragraph, for example, the sentences vary in length: a long, detailed sentence is followed by a short, crisp one. We also prompt our students to notice Twitchell's regular use of transitions, which help his readers to focus on his argument: "First," "And, second," "In fact," "of course," "Even today," and so on.

Topic 4, following the essay, provides a good topic for an essay of roughly 750 words. The last topic (7) provides a prompt for some in-class writing, before class discussion. Or, the sentences we ask students to explain can be assigned to groups of three or four students, again, before class discussion begins.

Elizabeth Cady Stanton
Declaration of Sentiments and Resolutions (p. 501)

Stanton's Declaration of 1848 is the historic precursor of the decade-long effort that finally failed in 1982 to enact a constitutional amendment for Equal Rights (ERA, as it was called). The Fourteenth Amendment, enacted twenty years after the Seneca Falls Convention, did provide that no state "shall . . . deprive any person of life, liberty, or property without due process of law, nor deny any person within its jurisdiction the equal protection of the laws." At face value, that might look like the rejection of gender as a basis for lawful discrimination. Opponents of ERA in the 1970s who professed sympathy with feminist claims for constitutional equality often pointed to the language quoted as if that settled the matter. Not so, however.

The term *male* entered the Constitution in the Fourteenth Amendment itself, thereby helping to etch more clearly the implicit and historic male bias of the Constitution and the laws from the beginning, and indicating that "due process" and "equal protection" were not to be given a gender-free reading. Lest there be any doubt on the matter, an Illinois case of 1873 settled it for decades. Arguing that she was entitled under the Fourteenth Amendment to be admitted to the bar, Myra Bradwell fought her case through the state courts to the U.S. Supreme Court, but to no avail. The language of the majority's decision enshrined in constitutional interpretation the worst excesses of male chauvinism (see *Bradwell v. Illinois* 83 U.S. 130 [1873]). Even the right to vote, demanded in the Seneca Falls Declaration in paragraph 4 ("elective franchise"), was not incorporated into the Constitution until 1920 (the Nineteenth Amendment). Full equality of the sexes under the laws and the Constitution, whether or not it is a good thing, still does not exist in our society.

Civil death (see paragraph 8) is the ultimate extreme to which a person can be reduced: denial by law of all civil rights, privileges, immunities, and liberties. (Not even prisoners on death row, today, suffer civil death.) Stanton elaborates the point (paragraphs 9–11). It was commonplace among feminists of the previous century to point out that marriage under law was functionally equivalent to civil death.

It was not, however, functionally equivalent to chattel slavery, which lasted another fifteen years after the Seneca Falls Convention. (Not surprisingly, the women who organized the Convention were staunch abolitionists.) It might be a useful classroom exercise for students to explore the differences under the law in the 1840s between the status of American white women, as the Declaration reports it, and the status of American black slaves. An excellent source for slave law is A. Leon Higginbotham Jr., *In the Matter of Color* (1978).

Melinda Ledden Sidak
Mob Mentality: Why Intellectuals Love *The Sopranos* (p. 506)

Most of the time, we are familiar with the material that we teach, but this essay is an exception. We have not seen a single episode of *The Sopranos* and know little about it other than the fact that it deals with a mob family and is extremely popular among TV viewers. Even worse, we confess that we have no interest in ever watching *The Sopranos*—a bad attitude perhaps, but one, alas, that we feel comfortable with.

Yet Sidak's essay has turned out to be one of our favorites for the classroom. In part that's because students find our ignorance of TV shows amusing, and related to this, because it gives them an opportunity for once to be the experts. Not all of your students will be devout followers of *The Sopranos*, but you'll discover that nearly all of them will know something about this show, or else that they will have some other show or shows they watch avidly and can talk about with enthusiasm.

And with insight too: it's striking that students who are uneasy about engaging in discussions about a literary work often are very adept when they describe the stories, characters, and themes of TV shows. We've found in fact that sometimes when we've managed to prompt a quiet or hesitant student to talk about a TV show, he or she may get a boost of confidence and as a result feel more inclined to risk speaking and asking questions about literary, political, and other kinds of selections.

Our procedure for working with Sidak's essay is fairly obvious. We begin by asking the class, "How many of you watch *The Sopranos*?" Right away, we make our confession: "I've never seen the show. . . . What's it about? Why is it so popular anyway?"

As the discussion unfolds, you might ask students to compare and contrast their views with those that Sidak presents. What is her argument? How effectively does she support it? Is her argument persuasive? From there, you can say this: "Well, some of you tell me you aren't fans of this show. Do you have other shows you like a lot?" As we noted, we are blissfully ignorant of everything that the students will be referring to. But there's an important lesson here that we are seeking to convey to the class, a lesson about the importance of "audience": how does one explain something to a reader or a listener who knows little or nothing about the topic? The students soon sense that they have to do some hard and careful work: they are *inside* an experience that the person they are communicating with is not inside at all. There's some laughter in the room, but also a feeling of struggle too, as students attempt to make us understand something they know a lot about and that we know next to nothing about.

"Keep your audience in mind" is, of course, one of those injunctions that all teachers of writing stress. No one disputes it. But it's not an easy thing to describe or achieve. It's hard enough to be clear to ourselves about what we mean. It's harder still to take the next step and make what is clear to us clear to our readers as well. What we want to communicate to students is that we write both for ourselves and for readers. In a piece of writing we are attempting to express and figure out something for ourselves even as we strive to share it with readers. Our readers cannot be asked to guess at what we mean: all that they have are the sentences that we write, and we have to be clear and accurate.

The special value, then, of Sidak's essay in the classroom is that as the students address us, they are obliged to be highly attentive to the problematic presence of their audience—the person standing in front of them is ready and willing to hear what they have to say but needs a lot of carefully presented information, background, and explanation. It's all clear to the students, but, so they quickly realize, it's by no means clear to their professor. The students thus have to get "outside" their own minds and imagine their way into the mind of (in this case at least) a benighted audience. It's a good challenge for them.

Stevie Smith
Not Waving but Drowning (p. 510)

All his life, the dead man had sent messages that were misunderstood. Even his efforts to mask his loneliness and depression were more successful than he intended. His friends mistook him for a "chap [who] always loved larking," as they now mistake the cause of his death. But true friends would have seen through the clowning, the dead man seems to protest, in lines 3 and 4 (when, of course, it is too late to protest or to explain). The second stanza confirms his view of the spectators. They are imperceptive and condescending; their understanding of the cause of his death is as superficial as their attention to him was while he was alive. But they didn't know him "all [his] life" (line 11). The dead man thus acknowledges, by leaving them out of the last stanza, that, never having risked honest behavior, he is at least as responsible as others for his failure to be loved and to love.

A Casebook on E-Mail

Nicholas Negroponte
Being Asynchronous (p. 511)

Negroponte uses a fair amount of jargon. His first sentence means something like this: "Conversations between people, whether they are face-to-face or on the telephone, take place with both parties participating and, for both, in the identical amount of time." In his second paragraph he writes of "off-line processing and time shifting" and "online discussion." Later, he writes of "interface agents [who] will use . . . bits to prioritize and deliver messages." At the same time, he intersperses these terms with ordinary phrases like "off-the-cuff exchanges" and messages that "would not stand a chance in hell" (of getting delivered). We can explain his diction in three ways. First, he is writing about some fairly new technical phenomena; second, he is explaining these phenomena to readers who have chosen to learn about them (by buying or borrowing his book *Being Digital*); and third, using jargon is fun: you speak swiftly and colorfully to folks who will respond in kind. We discourage students from using jargon inappropriately, but we find Negroponte's jargon appropriate.

Before you discuss the content of this article, we recommend that you explain to the students what the word "asynchronous" means. "Asynchronous": lack of temporal concurrence; absence of synchronism. "Synchronism" means:

1. Coincidence in time; simultaneous.

2. A chronological listing of historical personages or events so as to indicate parallel existence or occurrence.
3. Representation in the same artwork of events that occurred at different times.

Once you have done this, then we think you'll have some good responses to this question: "Why does Negroponte believe that 'E-mail is exploding in popularity'?"

You then might press the students a bit about Negroponte's point of view. He seems, on the one hand, to stress the advantages of e-mail, yet, on the other hand, his choice of words and phrasing imply its disadvantages as well. We have in mind, for example, his comment that "personal e-mail messages might drift to the top of the heap." That e-mails do indeed pile up on the screen—forming quite a "heap"—is a common complaint, and it is often expressed very vigorously, as in Rob Nixon's article later in this casebook.

The final line of Negroponte's article merits some notice—". . . the bizarre economic model behind it." Negroponte does not explain what he means, and we are not sure that we know what he is getting at ourselves. Perhaps he is suggesting that the economy in general runs on the basis of timing and scheduling, and that this economic model has been carried over to the world of leisure and entertainment—TV advertisers want to have access to lots of us at exactly the same time. But this may or may not be Negroponte's point—ask the students for their views. Nor does it help much to clarify why he uses the adjective "bizarre."

An interesting word, by the way. "Bizarre" means: strikingly unconventional and far-fetched in style or appearance; odd. It derives from the Spanish *bizarro*, brave, probably from Basque *bizar*, beard.

Judith Kleinfeld
Check Your E-Mail; You May Be Fired (p. 512)

Students respond well to "Check Your E-Mail," but we have found that it's better to begin class discussion with a specific question rather than a general one. The first time we taught this article, we started by asking: "Do you think that some kinds of bad news should not be delivered by e-mail?" There were some lively responses, and on one level the back-and-forth discussion was stimulating. But it soon seemed very scattered and all over the place. The question was too general, and the negative form ("should not be delivered") did not help.

Next time around, we began: "Do you think it is acceptable for a person to be 'fired through e-mail'?" That worked better; it gave the discussion and debate more focus. We then moved to a second question: "Do you think it is OK to break up with someone through e-mail?" Again, the gain was in the focus that a more directed question provides.

Our students pretty much agreed that it's fine (unpleasant, but OK) to be fired through e-mail but not to end a relationship through this means. From there, you might ask the students whether their responses suggest that a public matter is better suited to e-mail than a private one. They likely will say "yes," which can then lead you to query them about whether an e-mail is public or not. If you are fired, your coworkers will know the news soon enough. Does this mean that the message is a public one? But maybe it is preferable to receive the message on one's computer screen than to be called into the boss's office. Or would a "real" letter, delivered by the postman, be better still? A phone call—even better?

For fun, to change the rhythm, you might ask the students to do a little play-acting. Ask someone to play the boss and someone else to play an employee. Stage a scene or two where the employee is called in for the bad news. This is a nice way to dramatize the gains and losses, for both parties, of e-mail and face-to-face communication.

Rob Nixon
Please Don't E-Mail Me about This Article (p. 514)

This is an interesting article to discuss. It is written in a lively style, and Nixon acknowledges along the way the benefits of e-mail even as he inveighs against it. The problem with the article is that it records a complaint for which there is no remedy. Yes, there is too much e-mail; and, yes, it can be a huge pain in the neck. But, as Nixon says, it is very valuable for work; his research and teaching, he says, depend upon it. Nixon could not function professionally without e-mail; he would not really want to give it up. What he wants is what we all want: less e-mail, more control. But that is not going to happen.

This is roughly the sequence of questions we ask in class:

What is Nixon's point?
Does he believe that e-mail has some value?
Then why does he protest against it so vigorously?
Does he propose a solution?
Do you find this solution convincing?

The students we have taught admire the writing in Nixon's piece, but most of them shrug their shoulders in response to his complaint and to his weak notion that it's nice to get away from e-mail for a while. Students point to the obvious (which teachers know even more vividly): each day that e-mail is not answered means that the list of messages will be longer when the computer is finally turned back on again.

As we move to the end of the discussion, we ask students, "Is it worth it to write an article like this?" We are inclined to say that the answer is no, it's not. It describes a familiar feeling but ultimately goes nowhere with it because there's nothing really to be done about the situation that Nixon describes, and it is not clear that in truth he would want the situation to be different than it is.

Imagine saying to Nixon: "OK, you feel you are overwhelmed with e-mail. Starting tomorrow, your computer will be programmed to receive only five e-mails per day. All the others sent to you during that day will be automatically deleted." We doubt that Nixon would be happy with this, however much it would reduce his number of messages.

Ed Boland
In Modern E-Mail Romances "Trash" Is Just a Click Away (p. 517)

Here we offer the same suggestion that we made for the article in this casebook by Judith Kleinfeld: a more specific question is likely to be better than a general one. You could ask: "Why does the dating expert say that e-mail has 'changed every aspect of dating'?" This question will work; you'll receive plenty of responses. But you might be more effective if you proceed this way instead:

The dating expert whom Boland quotes says, "Our new technology is both boon and curse for the modern dater."

1. Why is it a boon?
2. Why is it a curse?

At this point we break the class into small groups so that the students can discuss together this topic:

Do you use e-mail for romance? What does it add to (or perhaps take away from) your interactions and relationships? Can you imagine romance without e-mail?

The students have plenty to say about this, but the discussion will be more free and open if it takes place among the students themselves, rather than with (that is, to) the teacher.

Besides, you may resemble us in finding such discussions a little awkward to lead and take part in. Turn things over to the students; they will enjoy being liberated from your presence for a while for some lively talk about a topic they have a keen interest in.

11

LAW AND ORDER

Illustrations

Bernie Boston
Flower Power (p. 522)

The place and time are the steps of the Pentagon in 1967. An antiwar marcher places carnations in the rifle barrels of army guards. The contrasts are obvious: flowers versus rifles, long hair versus dehumanizing helmets, softness versus hardness (the flowers, hair, and thick sweater; the helmets, brass insignia, and rifles), light versus dark.

Given the context here of law and order, it is appropriate to mention that the Supreme Court recognizes symbolic expression (such as protesting a war by wearing arm bands or by flying the flag upside down) as "speech" because such symbolism expresses an idea or emotion. Like verbal speech, it is protected by the First Amendment, subject to state regulation only if it threatens national security or public safety. The Court does, however, distinguish between "speech" (including nonverbal symbolic expression) and "speech plus," that is, speech accompanied by conduct such as parading or picketing, in which the physical movements are meant, more than the speech, to persuade the widest possible audience. The court has upheld the right of people to engage in "speech plus," but it has given the government the right to regulate the conduct to ensure the public safety. In this picture presumably the conduct is lawful, since placing flowers in rifle barrels can scarcely be imagined to interfere with the public safety.

Norman Rockwell
The Problem We All Live With (p. 523)

Norman Rockwell's name is not the household word that it was from, say, 1920 to 1970, but even today some of his pictures are reproduced on calendars, plates, and greeting cards.

Some students are likely to be familiar with Rockwell's work, and it can be useful to ask them to describe the pictures they recall and to compare those pictures with *The Problem*. For forty-seven years Rockwell painted sentimental anecdotal pictures of small-town America for the cover of *The*

Saturday Evening Post, but in 1963, when he was sixty-nine, he began working for *Look* (a magazine that folded a few years later), and he tackled some
new subjects that went beyond pathos and humor. *The Problem* appeared in
Look in 1964—the year of the Civil Rights Act that dealt with desegregating
the public schools. (In March 1963, lawsuits had been filed against three
school districts in Mississippi, a state in which no child attended an inte-
grated school. In September 1964, for the first time in Mississippi history,
African-American children—about fifty, all first-graders—attended white
public schools.)

Rockwell's art hitherto depicted a white-only world of corner barber-
shops, small parades, high school football games, elementary school classrooms, and humble repasts, though within this world there were usually
strong contrasts: youth and age, boys and girls, tears and laughter. His
people generally are very solemn or very genial; often they try to appear
solemn while overflowing with geniality, as when a family doctor obliges
a worried girl by putting a stethoscope to the chest of her doll. But in his
last fifteen years Rockwell sometimes turned to a world with problems
more serious than a doll's illness or a flat tire or a baseball batted through
a window. Here he turns to education—not just a cute kid all dressed up
and going off to college while his worried blue-collar dad and his morose
mutt wait with him for the bus—but the very structure of education in
America. Although in *The Problem* Rockwell is still in his small-town world
of nice little kids and big helpful adults, and he still uses his old device of
setting forth a contrast (here burly white deputy marshals and a small
African-American girl), the subject demands a new treatment. He most
unusually cuts off the top of the scene; ordinarily a Rockwell picture affec-
tionately records a bittersweet episode largely by letting us see the contrary expressions on the faces (glum dad, hopeful kid). Note too that here
the antagonist is shown only in the tomato that has fallen to the ground
after splattering on the wall behind the girl's head. Rockwell can't treat this
conflict in his usual way; he can't bring himself to show the ugliness of
mind that hurled the tomato. But Rockwell's pictorial solution to his problem (we are convinced that for him it was a problem to depict American
violence) is brilliant. The bits of tomato on the wall convey the violence—
and the stain becomes a sort of halo or star or fiery sun that enhances the
girl's dignity.

For a large reproduction of the picture, in color, see plate #550 in Thomas
S. Buechner, *Norman Rockwell* (1970).

Behind the picture, of course, is *Brown v. Board of Education,* the 1954 case
in which the Supreme Court ordered the desegregation of Washington
schools. The results of that decision are examined in several books that will
prove useful to students writing research papers on some aspect of desegregation. The following books give a variety of points of view: Raymond
Wolters, *The Burden of Brown: Thirty Years of School Desegregation* (1984); Jen-
nifer L. Hochschild, *The New American Dilemma: Liberal Democracy and School*

Desegregation (1984); Willis D. Hawley, *Strategies for Effective Desegregation* (1983); and Christine H. Rossell and Willis D. Hawley, eds., *The Consequences of School Desegregation* (1983).

Topic for Critical Thinking and Writing

What title would you give to the picture, and why? (The title bothers us. What is the problem? A superficial interpretation of the picture might suggest that African Americans are the problem; they want to attend the same schools that whites attend! But to such an interpretation one might well respond that the real problem is white racism. In short, we think the title, which was probably an editor's rather than Rockwell's, is unfortunate because it can easily be taken to suggest that African Americans are the "problem"; on the other hand, we think the picture, as opposed to the title, indicates that the problem is on the other side.)

Short Views

Topics for Critical Thinking and Writing

1. *Dr. Johnson and Boswell:* Despite the defeat of ERA, the law today guarantees women far more rights than it did in the eighteenth century. Still, students might be invited to speculate on the inherent powers of women. The second and longer passage that we give from Johnson strikes us as typical of his uncommon common sense. A noted criminal lawyer and professor of law, Alan M. Dershowitz, in *The Best Defense* (1982), says that defense lawyers are "an egotistical lot," and that their careers afford "a great ego trip" and (sometimes) lots of money, but he also says things along Johnson's line. Dershowitz's points: (1) it's the judge's or jury's job, not the lawyer's, to determine guilt; (2) even the guiltiest client is entitled to adequate defense; (3) the alternative is the Soviet system in which certain defendants are assumed not to be entitled to a lawyer; and (4) "it's important for lawyers to challenge the government in order to keep it honest. . . . The zealous defense attorney is the best bastion of liberty—the final barrier between an overreaching government and its citizens."

2. *Brandeis:* Despite Brandeis, public officials have usually enjoyed special status under the law. They are subject to criminal law, but if they violate a citizen's rights they are usually immune from lawsuits in which the aggrieved citizen seeks monetary compensation. The idea, according to a Supreme Court ruling of 1896, is that exposing officials to such civil actions "would seriously cripple the proper and effective administration of public affairs." In later rulings the Court has modified this view (for instance, if "malicious intent" can be proved), but in June 1982 the court ruled (in a case involving Richard Nixon) that presidents retain absolute immunity provided that they act within the "outer perimeters" of their official duties. The vote was 5–4; the dissenters argued that this ruling puts the president "above the law" and marks a reversion to the detestable doctrine that the king can do no wrong.

Thomas Jefferson
The Declaration of Independence (p. 527)

This document was addressed not to the King of Great Britain or to the English people but to the world ("mankind," in the first sentence), to the community of nations ("the powers of the earth"), and especially to France and Spain, from which the colonists expected help. That is, the Declaration does not appeal (as earlier revolutionaries in Britain did appeal) to the historical rights of Englishmen. Rather, appealing to a universal standard of human rights, it assures the world that the revolution is not an irresponsible upheaval but a principled action.

But of course the Declaration was also in a sense especially addressed to the British people, since the King—not the entire British government or the people—is made the villain. And the Declaration was also directed to the states themselves, for it is a pact between "these free and independent states."

The speakers are "the Representatives of the United States," who "hold these truths to be self-evident." That is, the speakers are reasonable and God-fearing men (they trust in Providence) who offer a thoughtful argument. They set forth principles at the start, then offer a catalog of facts, and then arrive at conclusions. Instructors who are teaching the techniques of persuasion will find the Declaration admirably suited to their purpose.

Herbert Aptheker, in *The American Revolution* (1960; Part II of his *History of the American People*), usefully points out that the enunciation of the colonists' cause has three basic parts: (1) human beings (essentially equal in attributes and needs) possess rights to life, liberty, and the pursuit of happiness; (2) to obtain these rights, they create government; (3) governments destructive to these rights are tyrannical and should be altered or abolished by the people, who then have the right and duty to create a government which (in the words of the Declaration) "to them shall seem most likely to effect their Safety and Happiness."

Once can put the argument this way:

> *Major premise*: Governments denying that men are created equal and are endowed with inalienable rights may be altered or abolished by the people, from whose consent the governments derive their just powers.
> *Minor premise*: The King has repeatedly acted tyrannically over the American states.
> *Conclusion*: The states may renounce allegiance to the King.

We have now touched on the first and fifth questions that we ask in the text. For the second question, on the revisions in the first part of the second paragraph, we offer a comment from Carl Becker's *The Declaration of Independence* (1942):

> When Jefferson submitted the draft to Adams the only correction which he made was to write "self-evident" in place of "sacred & undeniable." It is interesting to guess why, on a later reading, the other changes were made. I suspect that he erased "& independent" because, having introduced "self-evident," he did not like the sound of the two phrases both closing with "dent." The phrase "they are endowed by their creator" is obviously much better than "from that equal creation"; but this correction, as he first wrote it, left an awkward wording: "that they are endowed by their creator with equal rights some of which are inherent & inalienable among which are." Too many "which ares": and besides, why suppose that some rights given by the creator were inherent and some not? Thus we get the form, which is so much stronger, as well as more agreeable to the ear: "that they are endowed by their creator with inherent & inalienable rights." Finally, why say "the preservation of life"? If one has a right to life, the right to preserve life is manifestly included.

This passage from Becker's book, along with an extract from Aptheker's book as well as extracts from many other valuable sources, is given in *A Casebook on the Declaration of Independence*, edited by Robert Ginsberg. One other important source (published after Ginsberg's book) must be mentioned: Gary Wills, *Inventing America* (1978).

Topic for Critical Thinking and Writing

Write a persuasive Declaration of Independence for some imagined group. Examples: adolescents who declare that their parents have no right to govern them; young adolescents who declare that they should not be compelled to attend school; parents who declare that the state has no right to regulate the education of their children; college students who declare that they should not be required to take certain courses.

Henry David Thoreau
From "Civil Disobedience" (p. 531)

Your students may already know that Thoreau's essay was an important influence on, and inspiration for, Mohandas K. Gandhi and Martin Luther King Jr. in their reform campaigns. But we think it is valuable for students to see Thoreau's essay in its biographical and historical contexts, which we describe in our headnote. It's a timeless essay, a classic, but like all timeless works, it is nonetheless the result of—it is a response to—a specific moment in the writer's life and history.

We also remind students that Thoreau's act of civil disobedience, while courageous, was unusual for him. He was a staunch individualist, not really a social reformer; he believed that social life would inevitably become better as persons reformed themselves, and thus that the project of transforming individual hearts and minds should be the main focus. In this one instance, Thoreau took a moral stand against an unjust war, and he paid a price for it—though, to be honest, it was not much of a price, only a single night in the hometown jail. He never did anything as sustained, as difficult and demanding, as the work that Gandhi and King performed, work that took enormous effort and resolve over a span of many years.

If Thoreau was an activist, he was above all an activist through and in his writing. Thoreau loved the sheer act of writing, and he wrote constantly. Indeed, living at Walden Pond in the 1840s was for him less an immersion in nature than an opportunity for sustained literary labor, away from the busy family home with its boarders and pencil business. As soon as Thoreau arrived, he started composing two lectures about what he was doing and why.

He was hard at work all the time on essays and books, including a book about his stay at Walden (which hadn't yet ended), and he was generating page after page of journal entries and revising and reorganizing them. In *Walden* Thoreau chooses not to divulge how much time he spent at his writing desk, but in truth he was at Walden an indefatigable writer who was almost always writing. It's a wonder he had the time now and then to take a walk in the woods.

Thoreau lived only to age forty-four, yet he managed to write two major books (*A Week on the Concord and Merrimack Rivers* and *Walden*), many lectures and essays, thousands of pages of manuscript for other essays and books (a number of which were published after his death), thousands of more pages of notebooks, hundreds of poems, many letters, and millions of words in his journal. He lived to put pen to paper, and he made everyone and everything else secondary to that. Even nature, however dear it was to him, was in essence raw material for literary activity. Thoreau was possessed and driven by a will to write that few American authors have equaled.

We emphasize this fact about Thoreau in order to lead to a question we ask the students: Does "Civil Disobedience" stand on its own, or should we weigh and appraise it alongside the realities of the writer's most urgent commitments?—which, in Thoreau's case, was his writing. Yes, Thoreau took a stand, but do the arguments of "Civil Disobedience" suggest that he should have taken such stands more often than, in truth, he did? We then press the students (and ourselves) a bit: But is this question about, or, rather, criticism of, Thoreau really a fair one? Should we expect—can we expect—a person to be in his or her life completely faithful to the principles that Thoreau outlines? How do we know when we must resist an unjust law or practice, as opposed to a law or practice with which we disagree but which we judge to be tolerable?

Our best classes on "Civil Disobedience" have been a little messy and disorderly, with lots of questions raised and with issues debated and (usually) left unresolved. One problem with the essay, we have found, is that it is too easy for students to admire it. We think that they ought to admire it, but also that they should test and inquire into the grounds for their admiration and return to the text for a fresh look. For this reason, we always give the paper assignment on "Civil Disobedience" after the class has discussed it. This makes the essay harder for the students to write, but of course the advantage is that it requires them to think more analytically, to be more reflective about Thoreau's arguments and their own and others' responses to them.

The best recent discussion of Thoreau's essay is Lawrence A. Rosenwald's "The Theory, Practice, and Influence of Thoreau's 'Civil Disobedience'," in *A Historical Guide to Henry David Thoreau*, ed. William E. Cain (2000), pp. 153–179. Rosenwald concludes:

> Thoreau undogmatically sorted through all of the traditions available to him, rejecting what he could not use and holding fast what was good. The nonresistance of Garrison, Ballous, and Alcott, the revolutionary action of 1775, the Transcendentalist emphasis on conscience, the large historical events and small

personal accidents of Thoreau's own time, his mechanical expertise, and his masculine insecurity are all sifted for use in the essay. What has made the essay capable of exerting so great an influence is not only the severity of its idea but also its concreteness and unsystematic pragmatism. (p. 173)

Note: By "mechanical expertise," Rosenwald is referring to Thoreau's expert knowledge as a surveyor and as a scientist, including one who was involved in his family's pencil-making business; as Thoreau states in "Civil Disobedience," "Let your life be a counter friction to stop the machine."

For a stimulating essay on changing interpretations of "Civil Disobedience," see Evan Carton, "The Price of Privilege: 'Civil Disobedience' at 150," *The American Scholar* 67:4 (Autumn 1998):105–112. "Civil Disobedience," Carton contends,

exposes and undoes the psychological training that in one way or another we have all internalized. It dissolves the buffer between us and the host of distant sins that, in Thoreau's stunningly precise formulation, "from immoral have become, as it were, unmoral, and not quite unnecessary to that life which we have made." When we "just do it" in our Nikes, my students hear Thoreau whispering: Are you in fact doing it on the shoulders of the Indonesian (or now, because of a recent rise in the price of Indonesian labor, Vietnamese) sweatshop workers who make those Nikes for pennies an hour?

For a keen, accessible overview, we recommend Leo Marx, "The Struggle over Thoreau," *The New York Review of Books,* June 24, 1999. Biographies include Walter Harding, *The Days of Henry Thoreau* (1965; rev. ed., 1992), and Robert D. Richardson Jr., *Henry Thoreau: A Life of the Mind* (1986). For other teaching tips: Laraine Fergensen, "'Civil Disobedience' (or Is It 'Resistance to Civil Government'?) in a Composition Course," in *Approaches to Teaching Thoreau's* Walden *and Other Works,* ed. Richard J. Schneider (1996).

If time permits, you might bring to class some passages from Thoreau's later political essays, "Slavery in Massachusetts" (1854) and "A Plea for John Brown" (1859, 1860). Both of these essays are more violent in their rhetoric and more sympathetic toward violence as a form of social and political protest than is "Civil Disobedience." The best collections of Thoreau's writings are the two volumes in the Library of America Series, published in 1985 and 2001; the second contains the essays.

For cogent discussions of nonviolent and violent forms of "civil disobedience": Michael Martin, "Ecosabotage and Civil Disobedience," *Environmental Ethics* 12 (Winter 1990):291–310, and Gerald D. Coleman, "Civil Disobedience: A Moral Critique," *Theological Studies* 46 (March 1985):21–37.

Some of your students might enjoy examining the impact of Thoreau on Gandhi and King. See, for example, Manfred Steger, "Mahatma Gandhi and the Anarchist Legacy of Henry David Thoreau," *Southern Humanities Review,* 27:3 (Summer 1993), and Anita Haya Goldman, "American Philosophy as Praxis: From Emerson and Thoreau to Martin Luther King," *Salmagundi* 108 (Fall 1995).

Martin Luther King Jr.
Nonviolent Resistance (p. 535)

King's discussion is an admirable example of analysis, classifying the ways in which victims deal with oppression. But it is also an admirable example of persuasive writing. Indeed, as King makes clear in the third paragraph from the end, his subject in part is "persuasion." Of course, the lucidity of the analysis is itself a persuasive element, but King uses other techniques too.

Note, for instance, in the first paragraph the allusions to the Bible and to Shakespeare (the speaker establishes himself as one who knows history and who knows the great thoughts of the past); and note that although the first way of dealing with oppression is scarcely noble, the speaker does not speak contemptuously of the victims. Rather, he sympathetically quotes an anonymous guitarist, and we feel that he understands this man's response. He cannot approve of it (note the decisive "But this is not the way out" at the beginning of the third paragraph), but he has won our sympathy as a man of intelligence, goodwill, and understanding. We must, King reminds us in the third paragraph, be our brother's keeper (an echo of Genesis 4.9), and he continues to hold our interest and our esteem, never alienating us with a holier-than-thou attitude. Always there is the note of sincerity, emphasized by apparently simple sentences ("It is the way of the coward") and by repetition (for instance, "his brother's keeper" and "the Negro cannot win," both repeated in the third paragraph). Note, too, that the exhortation to blacks to adopt nonviolent resistance is at the end set in a context that is reassuring to whites, for King is speaking to blacks and to whites. Fundamentally his topic is not black power but justice, and his last paragraphs argue that it is not enough for there to be law: "the law needs help. . . . In the end, for laws to be obeyed, men must believe they are right."

The sentence that we have just quoted prompts us to offer a brief note on civil disobedience. Presumably most persons who practice civil disobedience hope that their willingness to accept subsequent prosecution will draw public attention to what they believe to be an immoral law. Government has the legitimate right to punish such persons, but if their position is morally compelling, as King's was, the conscience of the majority will be touched and the law will be changed. Thus civil disobedience is not a sign that government is collapsing; rather it may be a legitimate part of the process of forming law.

It is worth mentioning, too, that although persons who today engage in civil disobedience are usually associated with causes regarded as leftist, the political right also has advocated civil disobedience. On August 10, 1988, the Reverend Jerry Falwell praised antiabortion picketers in Atlanta for making the "same sacrifice" that civil rights demonstrators had made in the 1960s. On the following day he urged his followers in New Orleans to engage in widespread "civil disobedience." "This is a departure from anything I've ever preached," he said. "The only way [to get Congress to pass an antiabortion amendment to the Constitution] is nonviolent civil disobedience."

Topics for Critical Thinking and Writing

1. On the basis of the persona in this selection, characterize Dr. King in a paragraph.

2. Identify and evaluate Dr. King's chief persuasive techniques.

Martin Luther King Jr.
Letter from Birmingham Jail (p. 539)

King's letter was prompted by a letter (printed in the text) by eight Birmingham clergymen. His letter is unusually long ("Never before have I written so long a letter") because he was jailed at the time and thus was unable to speak to audiences face-to-face.

King goes to some length to show that his work is thoroughly in the American (and Judeo-Christian) tradition. That is, although he rebuts the letter of the eight clergymen, he represents himself not as a radical, nor in any way un-American (and of course not as an opponent of the Judeo-Christian tradition), but as one who shares the culture of his audience. Thus, although he rejects the clergymen's view that he is impatient, he begins by acknowledging their decency. They are, he says, "men of genuine good will"—and in saying this King thereby implies that he too is a man of good will. Moreover, King's real audience is not only the eight clergymen but all readers of his letter, who are assumed to be decent folk. Notice, too, in his insistence that he is speaking on an issue that involves all Americans, his statement (paragraph 4) that "Injustice anywhere is a threat to justice everywhere." But his chief strategy early in the letter is to identify himself with Paul (paragraph 3) and thus to guide his mainly Christian audience to see him as carrying on a tradition that they cherish. Notice also the references to Niebuhr, Buber (a Jew), and Jesus.

It is usual, and correct, to say that King is a master of the appeal to emotion. This essay reveals such mastery, as in paragraph 14, when he quotes a five-year-old boy: "Daddy, why do white people treat colored people so mean?" And because King is really addressing not so much the eight clergymen as a sympathetic audience that probably needs encouragement to persist rather than reasons to change their beliefs, an emotional (inspirational) appeal is appropriate. But the essay is also rich in lucid exposition and careful analysis, as in paragraph 6 (on the four steps of a nonviolent campaign) and paragraphs 15–16 (comparing just and unjust laws).

Topics for Critical Thinking and Writing

1. Think of some injustice that you know something about, and jot down the facts as objectively as possible. Arrange them so that they form an outline. Then, using these facts as a framework, write an essay (possibly in the form of a letter to a specific audience) of about 500 words, presenting your case in a manner somewhat analogous to King's. For example, don't hesitate to make comparisons with biblical, literary, or recent historical material, or to use personal experiences, or to use any other persuasive devices you wish, including appeals to the emotions. Hand in the objective list along with the essay.

2. If some example of nonviolent direct action has recently been in the news, such as actions by persons who oppose nuclear power plants, write an essay evaluating the tactics and their effectiveness in dealing with the issue.

Cathy Booth Thomas
A New Scarlet Letter (p. 554)

Some students will recognize the allusion in the title; some may even have read Hawthorne's *The Scarlet Letter* (1850). Apparently the earliest record of an adulterer being required to wear a badge or embroidered letter is found in the *Plymouth Colonial Records* of 1639: "The Bench doth therefore censure the said Mary . . . to wear a badge upon her left sleeve." The letter in Hawthorne's title is "A," standing for adulterer; it is done in gold embroidery on a scarlet background, scarlet of course standing for unbridled passion.

The gist of the issue today is not adultery but other offenses. Is it appropriate to label—literally to label, with a sign perhaps on the person's lawn or automobile—a wrongdoer such as a child-molester, or a drunk driver, much as Hawthorne's Hester Prynne was labeled as an adulterer? This issue surely can produce interesting arguments on both sides, and we would have no hesitation assigning it. Further, beyond the basic issue of whether or not this sort of punishment is acceptable, there is the issue of this particular judge's methods.

In teaching this essay we would spend most of our time on issues concerning argument, but in *LBR* we could not resist calling attention (in our second question) to the tone of the first sentence: "Gabriel Trevino did a bad, bad thing." In the next sentence we learn that the "bad thing" was that "he fondled the 14-year-old daughter of a friend." Obviously the first sentence is meant to be amusing—it is the voice of a parent speaking to a naughty child—but our question seeks to cause students to think about whether it is acceptable to be playful when one is talking about this very serious issue. Is this issue something that one can kid about? Does the writer, by adopting the tone she does, imply that the issue is not so serious as we think it is?

Ordinarily we like to see writers use language engagingly, for instance, to create an interesting voice, but this particular example disturbs us. Gabriel Trevino's action was not that of a child eating a forbidden cookie. Even if one takes the view that some fourteen-year-old youths may be sexually mature and may even be mentally mature enough to understand the implications of sexual activity, in this instance it seems clear that an adult was taking advantage of a child.

Michael Chabon
Solitude and the Fortresses of Youth (p. 557)

Is it true that "it is in the nature of a teenager to want to destroy"? As they say in some instructors' manuals, "Answers will vary." We can think of writers at one extreme, such as Hobbes ("The condition of man . . . is a condition of war of everyone against everyone," and "The secret thoughts of a man run over all things, holy, profane, clean, obscene, grave, and light, without shame or blame"), and we can also think of writers at the other extreme, such as Rousseau ("Man is by nature good. . . . Men are depraved and perverted by society").

Well, let's assume there is at least a bit of truth in Hobbes's view about our secret thoughts, and let's assume that some writing expresses our darker side. What of it? Can one argue that writing of the sort that got the young man expelled from college is perhaps cathartic, i.e., that the *expression* of such thoughts serves a useful, healthful purpose? Conceivably a young man (or an old man, for that matter) who writes about, say, rape and other forms of violence thereby finds a harmless outlet for his feelings and fantasies and thus does *not* put them into action.

One might also consider the issue of whether such material may be published, and, if it is published, whether it may stimulate readers to acts of violence. Today, when almost anything can be published—or can appear on TV—it is hard to remember that there was a time, not so long ago, when Joyce's *Ulysses* and Lawrence's *Lady Chatterley's Lover* were banned. It is easy for us to be amused when we read that these books will corrupt people, but the fact is that they did seem dangerous to many guardians of public morality. Probably almost no one today disapproves of such books—their offense was that they talked explicitly about sex—but plenty of people today strongly disapprove of representations of certain kinds of violence, and indeed one does occasionally read in the newspapers that some kid engaged in a violent act because he saw it depicted in what we still call a comic book even though there is nothing funny in many of these publications.

Are representations of violence—stabbings, rape, throwing bodies out of windows—to be censored because some individual may be moved to imitate them? Again, "Answers will vary," but our own response is rooted in Judge

Woolsey's famous decision in the *Ulysses* case, where he said that the test of whether a work is obscene is the response of the *ordinary* person, not the unusual person who may indeed engage in some notably unsocial act after reading something in a book. (Woolsey's decision is reprinted in the Modern Library edition of *Ulysses*.)

A final note: our fourth question asks students to comment on Chabon's final paragraph. Why? Because we fear that some of them may not at first recognize that he is being ironic.

If you assign this essay, you may want to relate it to an essay that appears earlier in the book, Richard Rhodes's "Hollow Claims about Fantasy Violence," in Chapter 4.

Chesa Boudin
Making Time Count (p. 560)

Chesa Boudin's first sentence is straightforward and clear, and it seizes the reader's attention. From start to finish, our students find this piece a compelling one; for most of them, Boudin is describing an experience from which they are far removed, even as they can feel its painful impact. But when you introduce the essay, you might keep in mind the possibility that some of your students know someone—it could be a family member—who has been or who is in prison. The first time we taught this selection, we approached it by assuming that Boudin was telling about a situation no one in the class would have direct knowledge of. Without going into details, we can report that this was not the case. This made us realize yet again—a lesson that many of us as teachers find hard to remember—that much more may be going on in the lives of students than we realize. Something we may believe is distant from their lives and experiences often turns out to be intimately close.

In several places, Boudin refers to the importance of language—the language of adoption and divorce, for example, which makes a child unsure about how to refer to important persons in his or her life. Is this my mother, or my biological mother? Is she my mother, or my adoptive mother, or both? Who is my real mother? For students in our courses, quite a few of whom have experienced the separation and divorce of their parents, or whose biological parents may have remarried, or who may be adopted and who may or may not know who their biological parents are—these and related issues bring with them a host of challenges that involve names, identities, and terms, as Boudin indicates.

Notice also Boudin's discussion of phone calls, letters, stories, and, later, lies. Here again, you can explore the issues he considers while you highlight how these are bound up with significant (and awkward and wounding, and sometimes consoling and revealing) uses of language.

When we examine this essay in class as a piece of writing, we like to point out Boudin's effective use of paragraphing. Focus, for example, on the opening of paragraphs 5 and 11. Paragraphing, we think, is a valuable element of good writing, and one perhaps that teachers and students do not stress enough.

We suggest to our students that they keep their paragraphs a "good" length—by which we mean, not too long, not too short. Don't give readers in a single paragraph more than they can absorb, but do not give them too little, a point or an insight that is only touched on, not developed.

Of course, from a different direction, we also encourage students to aim for some variety in their paragraphing. Not too long, not too short—that's the basic rule. But for the sake of the reader's eye and ear, seek as well to vary the length of paragraphs a bit. Aim for some shifts and modulations of the rhythm of the essay.

It's possible, however, to do even more with paragraphing, as Boudin's essay illustrates. The first sentence in a new paragraph can give a special emphasis to the point that the paragraph will present, and it can also intensify the transition being made to *this* paragraph from the one that precedes it. Conceive of your paragraphing, we say to students, as a *strategy*.

Good paragraphing is indeed a strategy. It is a strategic resource for good writing. In particular it's something to look for, and to develop and hone, during the "revision" stages of work on an essay.

Derek Bok
Protecting Freedom of Expression on the Campus (p. 566)

In his title Bok pretty much reveals his position, but we think it is worth calling to the attention of the class that he does not (aside from the title) begin by vigorously announcing his thesis. Instead, in the first paragraph he gives the essential background (two students displayed Confederate flags, and another displayed a swastika), and in the second he tells us that "These incidents have provoked much discussion and disagreement." The rest of the second paragraph is devoted to summarizing the two sides ("Some students. . . . Others. . . .").

The point of all this, and of the next few paragraphs, is to establish Bok as a thoughtful person, someone who is trying to see things clearly and trying to make important distinctions (paragraph 4 begins, "It is important to distinguish. . . ."). In paragraph 4 Bok states his position unambiguously (he believes that "speech is protected by the First Amendment"), but even as he sets forth his defense of speech he expresses regret that the students engaged in certain speech (in this case the display of flags, which comes under the heading of speech). The total effect, again, is of a thoughtful person, a person who is aware of the sensibilities of others and who sees the damage that speech can do but who nevertheless believes it is essential to protect speech. And of course by the end of his essay Bok has suggested that banning speech is in the long run less effective than educating people by means of open discussion.

Our first question in the text, suggesting that the display of a swastika or a Confederate flag can be (for some people) "equivalent to a slap in the face, . . . an act of violence," took its origin from a letter by Martin Kilson, a member of Bok's faculty. Kilson wrote (March 31, 1991) to *The Boston Globe*:

> Occasionally you have to rethink the boundaries between free speech and speech that harms. When the Nazis march in Skokie, Il., before hundreds of Jews whose relatives have died in the Holocaust—that's no longer free speech, in my view. That's violence.

Kilson may be glancing at the "fighting words" doctrine, set forth by the Supreme Court in the 1942 Chapinsky case. This held that hateful epithets hurled at individuals are not protected; they can be conceived of as violence, aimed at provoking violence. Thus (as we understand it), if one says to a Wisian, "You are another of those treacherous Wisians," a court may find that the speech is not protected since no true Wisian can be expected to tolerate such an assault. On the other hand, the court's interpretation of "fighting words" does not include words addressed to groups. One can with impunity say to a group, for instance, in a lecture, "The Wisians are all a bunch of traitors and they are responsible for the mess we are in." Here the idea is that because no individual is singled out, and because the words are delivered in a public forum, no Wisian can reasonably get so inflamed that he or she is naturally impelled to strike back. The lecture may deeply offend those Wisians present, but the circumstances sufficiently cool the situation, making the words less than "fighting words," and therefore the words are protected.

As we imply in question 3, many colleges and universities have developed speech codes, sometimes on the grounds that an educational institution is a community of people united in the pursuit of learning and that obnoxious and harassing speech may make it impossible for some members of the community effectively to concentrate on their studies. The courts, however, have declared some of these codes unconstitutional. For instance, the University of Wisconsin's disciplinary code said that "jokes that have the purpose of making the educational environment hostile" are barred. A federal judge overturned the rule. The University of Michigan's code prohibited verbal and physical behavior that stigmatized individuals on the basis of race, ethnicity, religion, sex, sexual orientation, creed, national origin, age, or physical handicap. A Michigan pamphlet gave the following example of unacceptable speech: "A male student makes remarks in his class like 'women just aren't as good in this field as men.'" This code too was overturned, the judge ruling that the university cannot proscribe such speech even if it causes great anxieties on the campus. Again, the courts protect all public speech (e.g., the utterances of a lecturer or a newspaper editorial), and a number of colleges and universities in their codes make this point, prohibiting only face-to-face verbal assaults on individuals.

Michael Levin
The Case for Torture (p. 569)

Torture has not received positive press in recent decades, even though it continues to be widely practiced as an interrogation technique in many parts of the world. As the social philosopher Henry Shue has noted, "No other practice except slavery is so universally and unanimously condemned in law and human convention." To which the authors of Amnesty International's *Report on Torture* (1975) added: "At the same time the practice of torture has reached epidemic proportions." Indeed, after the attack on the World Trade Center, September 11, 2001, a number of talk-show hosts raised the issue of whether torture would be acceptable if there were very strong reasons to believe that a given individual had information that, if known to others, could avert such a disaster. We ourselves heard more than one person assert that although torture is a Very Bad Thing, in some circumstances it is the lesser of two evils and might well be chosen.

Identifying torture as a human-rights violation did not rise to the level of international human-rights law until after World War II. The basis for all later international prohibitions is Article 5 of the Universal Declaration of Human Rights (1948), which declares that "No one shall be subjected to torture or to cruel, inhumane or degrading treatment or punishment." The same language appears in Article 7 of the International Covenant on Civil and Political Rights (1976). Under the authority of the United Nations Convention against Torture and Other Cruel, Inhuman or Degrading Treatment or Punishment (1984), a special U.N. Committee against Torture has been established. How effective these provisions have been in suppressing torture and punishing torturers is another matter.

No doubt the principal current source of popular awareness of and opposition to torture is Amnesty International, whose Campaign for the Abolition of Torture began in 1972 and continues to the present.

Hypothetical cases to the side (questions 1 and 2), we have difficulty accepting the criterion Levin offers (which we quote) to demark the justified from the unjustified use of torture. How many innocent lives need to be saved before torture is justified? Levin does not tell us (how could he?). Above all, how do we avoid the all-too-obvious slippery slope: Once we openly allow torture in the kinds of cases Levin accepts, how are we to keep others from loosening the criteria to include persons "very probably" guilty? Or applying the criteria on the basis of an imperfect grasp of the relevant facts? Or turning prematurely to torture when other possibly effective interrogation methods might work? To us, Levin seems remarkably complacent about this nest of problems.

On the other hand, we are reluctant to embrace an absolute human right forbidding torture. Candor requires us to admit that we have no better alternative to offer for the kind of hypothetical cases Levin conjures up. (Again, the disaster in New York City on September 11, 2001, might make a sort of test case.) Levin's cases have been designed in such a way that it is all but impossible to reject his conclusion. What one can say is that his hypothetical cases bear little relation to the kinds of cases in which we know torturers today and in the past have done their work.

In addition to Amnesty's *Report on Torture* (1975), two other books might be mentioned because of the light they shed on the actual use of torture—a story quite remote from the considerations that inspire Levin's defense. One is Edward Peters, *Torture* (1985), a historical survey of torture from Greek and Roman times to the recent past. The other is *The Breaking of Bodies and Minds* (1985), edited by Eric Stover and Elena O. Nightingale, full of stories of recent vintage that record the terrors of those at the mercy of torturers.

George Orwell
Shooting an Elephant (p. 572)

In the second paragraph of "Shooting an Elephant" Orwell explicitly tells us that his experience as a police officer in Burma was "perplexing and upsetting." He characterizes himself as "young and ill-educated" at the time (clearly in the past) and says he was caught between his hatred of imperialism and his rage against the Burmese. The essay's paradoxical opening sentence foreshadows its chief point (that imperialism destroys the freedom of both the oppressor and the oppressed), but Orwell devotes the rest of the first paragraph, with its ugly characterizations of the Burmese, to dramatizing his rage. Students unaware of Orwell's preoccupation with decency (and unaccustomed to holding more than one paragraph in their heads at the same time) may fail to understand that the first two paragraphs do not contradict but reinforce each other. The racial slurs in the first paragraph, and elsewhere in the essay, are deliberate and show the alienation from normal feelings, the violations of self which were, as Orwell goes on to show, the by-products of his role. That he was playing a role is highlighted by the theatrical metaphors that accumulate in the seventh paragraph. (About to shoot the elephant, he sees himself as a "conjurer" with a "magical rifle," as an "actor," and as "an absurd puppet.") The essay's final paragraph, with its cold tone, its conflicting half-truths and rationalizations, again effectively dramatizes the deadening of feeling and loss of integrity Orwell experienced and that he believes all who turn tyrant experience.

John
The Woman Taken in Adultery (p. 578)

As we say in our headnote, most scholars agree that this story, which is not found in the earliest Greek manuscripts, is not really part of the Gospel According to St. John but is an account that somehow got inserted into late manuscripts. On grounds of diction it is said to resemble Luke far more than John.

The Mosaic law required that an adulterer be put to death (Lev. 20.10, Deut. 22.22), but it scarcely required the scribes and Pharisees to be so callous toward the woman or so eager to trip Jesus. They hoped to force Jesus to reject the Mosaic law; or, alternatively, possibly they sought to make him vulnerable to a charge (by Roman authorities) that he incited people to murder the woman. Note how they use the woman for their own purposes:

> And the scribes and Pharisees brought unto him a woman taken in adultery; and when they had set her in the midst, they say unto him, "Master, this woman was taken in adultery, in the very act. Now Moses in the law commanded us that such should be stoned: but what sayest thou?

That business of setting her in the midst and of specifying "in the very act" has an ugly sound. To our ear, the King James Version, which puts the words at the end of the sentence and thereby gives them emphasis, is far superior to the Revised Standard Version.

The scribes and Pharisees "continued asking him," pressing for an answer that would damage him. Jesus's unexplained gesture of writing on the ground can never be decisively explained, but perhaps it indicates his distress (which he seeks to relieve by a physical distraction) at seeing and hearing this malicious spectacle. A second interpretation, not incompatible with what we have just said, is that the episode keenly involves the readers, making us wonder what Jesus's words might have been. But in time he answers. His response does not mean that he dismisses the sin of adultery as trivial; it does mean, however, that he refuses to condemn the woman and that he sees in the scribes and Pharisees behavior at least as sinful, which ought to teach them to temper justice with mercy. His words strike home: The judges are "convicted by their own conscience." Note that Jesus bids the woman to give up her sinful life. He does not always speak so gently to sinners, and so we must assume that here he perceived she was not fixed in evil but was contrite.

The exact lesson can be much debated, but we think *The Jerome Biblical Commentary* (1968) gives a summary (p. 441 in the portion of the book devoted to the New Testament) to which many readers can subscribe. It says:

> The lesson of the story is, of course, not that sin is of no importance, nor that God does not punish sin, but that God extends mercy to the sinner that he may turn from his sin. The picture of the sinner and the Sinless standing face to face exem-

plifies the call to repentance. Thus, though Jesus himself does not judge (8.15), it is nevertheless for judgment that he has come into the world (9.39).

One final point: this episode is the only place recorded in the New Testament where Jesus confronts the issue of legal execution. Does the episode suggest that devout Christians must oppose the death penalty?

Mitsuye Yamada
To the Lady (p. 579)

First, some background. In 1942 the entire Japanese and Japanese-American population on America's Pacific coast—about 112,000 people—was incarcerated and relocated. More than two-thirds of the people moved were native-born citizens of the United States. (The 158,000 Japanese residents of the Territory of Hawaii were not affected.)

Immediately after the Japanese attack on Pearl Harbor, many journalists, the general public, Secretary of the Army Henry Stimson, and congressional delegations from California, Oregon, and Washington called for the internment. Although Attorney General Francis Biddle opposed it, on February 19, 1942, President Franklin D. Roosevelt signed Executive Order 9066, allowing military authorities "to prescribe military areas . . . from which any or all persons may be excluded." In practice, no persons of German or Italian heritage were disturbed, but Japanese and Japanese Americans on the Pacific coast were rounded up (they were allowed to take with them "only that which can be carried") and relocated in camps. Congress, without a dissenting vote, passed legislation supporting the evacuation. A few Japanese Americans challenged the constitutionality of the proceeding, but with no immediate success.

Although anti-Japanese sentiment is currently on the rise, it may be difficult for some students to comprehend the intensity of anti-Japanese sentiment that pervaded the 1940s. Here is a sample, sent to us by David Mura. Lt. General John DeWitt, the man in charge of the relocation plan, said:

> The Japanese race is an enemy race and while many second and third generation Japanese born on United States soil, possessed of United States citizenship, have become "Americanized," the racial strains are undiluted. To conclude otherwise is to expect that children born of white parents on Japanese soil sever all racial affinity and become loyal Japanese subjects. . . . Along the vital Pacific Coast over 112,000 potential enemies, of Japanese extraction, are at large today. There are indications that these are organized and ready for concerted action at a favorable opportunity. The very fact that no sabotage has taken place to date is a disturbing and confirming indication that such action will be taken.

One rubs one's eyes in disbelief at the crazy logic that holds that because "no sabotage has taken place . . . such action will be taken." By the way, not a single Japanese American was found guilty of subversive activity. For two good short accounts, with suggestions for further readings, see the articles entitled "Japanese-Americans, wartime relocation of," in *Kodansha Encyclopedia of Japan*, 4:17–18, and "War Relocation Authority," in 8:228.

It may be interesting to read Yamada's poem aloud in class, without having assigned it for prior reading, and to ask students for their responses at various stages—after line 4, line 21, and line 36. Lines 1–4 pose a question that perhaps many of us (young and old, and whether of Japanese descent or not) have asked, at least to ourselves. The question, implying a criticism of the victims, shows an insufficient awareness of Japanese or Japanese-American culture of the period. It also shows an insufficient awareness of American racism; by implying that protest by the victims could have been effective, it reveals ignorance of the terrific hostility of whites toward persons of Japanese descent.

The first part of the response shows one aspect of the absurdity of the lady's question. Japanese and Japanese Americans were brought up not to stand out in any way (certainly not to make a fuss) and to place the harmony of the group (whether the family or society as a whole) above individual expression. Further, there was nothing that these people could effectively do, even if they had shouted as loudly as Kitty Genovese did. For the most part they were poor, they had no political clout, and they were hated and despised as Asians. The absurdity of the view that they could have resisted effectively is comically stated in "should've pulled myself up from my / bra straps" (echoing the red-blooded American ideal of pulling oneself up by one's bootstraps), but of course the comedy is bitter.

12

CONSUMING DESIRES

Illustrations

Grant Wood
American Gothic (p. 582)

The pose in this painting (1930) is frontal, like those in an amateur's snap-shot of the family, and the faces display the seriousness of ordinary people who are uneasy at the attention being paid to them but who are doing their best to rise to the occasion. The man stares fixedly at the "camera"; his recti-tude will not allow him to put on an act. The woman (deferentially standing a bit behind her husband, of course) is a trifle more compliant, softening the pose by turning her head slightly. Both figures convey strength and honesty. They are utterly harmonious with each other, with their work and their cloth-ing and their Carpenter Gothic home: the shape of the pitchfork (a reminder of life lived close to the soil) reappears in the man's coveralls, in the house's windows and siding, and (less emphatically) in the lower part of the man's face and in the rickrack of the woman's apron. A variation of the pattern on the apron reappears in the upper window. The meticulous detail in the paint-ing tells us not only of the scrupulous effort that these two people exert but also of the painter's admiration for their way of life. By the way, Wood intended the figures to be a father and his spinster daughter (the pitchfork was supposed to be a threat to suitors), but no one ever sees it this way.

For a brilliant discussion of the technology behind the picture—the con-struction of the house, the origin of the bib-overall and of the bamboo sunscreen at the left, and other details—see Guy Davenport's essay, "The Geography of the Imagination," in his book (1981) with that title. Virtually all commentators on the picture point out its resemblance (in pose and in meticulous finish) to Flemish painting, for example, to van Eyck's double portrait of the Arnolfini, but so far as we know, only Davenport points out the resemblance to Egypt-ian sculpture of pharaohs and their wives. For an essay emphasizing Ameri-can sources of the painting (photography, fiction, etc.), see Wanda Corn's essay in *Art, the Ape of Nature*, edited by Moshe Barasch and Lucy Freeman.

Richard Hamilton
Just what is it that makes today's homes so different, so appealing? (p. 583)

This collage is fiendishly ingenious. It must have been easy enough to clip pictures of furniture, gadgets, and people out of magazines. But to get pictures whose scale was compatible must have been difficult. How, for example, to include the comic page, perhaps second only to TV as a source of values for the child and the childlike? Almost surely it would be impossible to find an image small enough to fit in the hand of either of the two people in the collage. Hamilton solved the problem by treating one segment of a comic strip as a large picture hanging on a wall. The ceiling, by the way, is a photograph of the earth taken from a high-altitude rocket, and the rug is a photograph of hundreds of people at a beach.

The collage, then, made up chiefly of clippings from popular magazines, is a presentation of the things that make today's homes "so different, so appealing." One may at first assume that this phrase is ironic and that Hamilton shares the liberal or humanistic contempt for the deplorable taste of the unenlightened. But judging from Hamilton's writings and other work, and from the work of other pop artists, that assumption is too easy. Hamilton, the father (better, the daddy) of pop art, delights in mass culture, which after all is a combination of popular taste and advanced technology. Hamilton says that he likes things that are mass produced, gimmicky, expendable, and sexy. But primarily he likes communication; he is fascinated with the ways in which advertisements communicate (drawings, photographs, and words can coexist in a single ad, to make a point), and in his art he uses modern techniques of communication.

Our experience suggests, however, that here he fails to communicate his message since most viewers take the picture to be a criticism of modern life rather than a celebration of it. The narcissism of the two figures (surely they are incapable of loving anyone but themselves), the abundance of gadgets, and the disproportionately long staircase—all are unnerving. Still, it is indisputable that the picture also delights, and so perhaps Hamilton does succeed in communicating his enthusiasm after all.

Topic for Critical Thinking and Writing

Read what you can find by and about Richard Hamilton. Then analyze the collage and explain what Hamilton finds so appealing about popular culture. (*A note to instructors:* Material on Hamilton can be found by consulting *Art Index*, especially by following leads on pop art, or the Web.)

Short Views

Topics for Critical Thinking and Writing

1. In the text we begin with a Chinese proverb ("Heaven is not as high as the desires of the human heart") and we go on to quote comparable pithy sayings (e.g., "You are what you eat"). Ask students to contribute comparable bits of folklore and to examine the degree to which the sayings ring true.

2. *Diane White*: Ask students if it is true that "It's difficult to have respect for a fast food cheeseburger." And what kinds of food *do* command respect? Or, when we eat, is it the particular situation, not the food, that commands respect?

3. *Le Corbusier*: Le Corbusier was certainly *not* saying that we should live mechanically—some students take the sentence this way—but rather that the house should serve as, just as a machine (e.g., the automobile) should serve us, i.e., it should help us to live better, happier lives.

Peter Farb and George Armelagos
The Patterns of Eating (p. 586)

Although the paragraphs are on the long side and the pace is unrelenting, this essay will cause no difficulties for students. It conveys an enormous amount of information that is likely to be new to them (e.g., that forks were scarcely known before the sixteenth century), but this information is easily grasped. In fact, beneath the abundant engaging details are generalizations that are offered so briefly and so matter-of-factly that one hardly stops to question them. An example is the statement (paragraph 3) that "Once the spontaneous, direct, and informal manners of the Middle Ages had been repressed, people began to feel shame" at acts of defecation and urination. This assertion is made as matter-of-factly as the statement that forks appeared in the late Middle Ages.

The essay provides ample opportunities for students from countries other than the United States to talk about their customs—and (more important, from our point of view) to *write* about them.

Topics for Critical Thinking and Writing

1. Find a reproduction of a painting by Norman Rockwell showing a family at a festive meal. Describe and analyze the painting, comparing Rockwell's image

with an image in your mind's eye of a "real" (contemporary) family at a similar meal.

2. Farb and Armelagos say, in their second sentence, that table manners "reveal the attitudes typical of a society." If you are familiar with two societies, compare the table manners and indicate what they reveal.

David Gerard Hogan
Fast Food (p. 590)

For most students, fast food consists of hamburgers, french fries, hot dogs, and pizza. And most do not share the criticisms of fast food that Hogan lists, among them increased litter and the exploitation of teenage workers. As Hogan says, in his fourth paragraph, "Fast food remains central to the American diet because it is inexpensive, quick, convenient, and predictable, and because it tastes good." He might have added "and because it is heavily advertised on TV and in magazines." In his sixth paragraph Hogan writes, "Some detractors claim that it [fast food] is even deliberately used by the United States, as a tool of cultural imperialism." He offers no support for that claim and concedes a few sentences later that the "rapid spread of American fast food is . . . more the result of aggressive corporate marketing strategies."

Many students have worked or currently work for fast food companies, and you can invite them to recount their experiences at work and their opinions of fast food, in class discussion or in an essay of roughly 750 words. Students who have traveled abroad, as many have, might be asked to write about their observations of a McDonalds in Paris or a KFC or Taco Bell in Shanghai. How did they feel about finding these familiar landmarks abroad? More important, how satisfied with American fast food were the French or Chinese customers whom they observed?

Hogan's article discloses many indictments of fast food, contrasting sharply with Maurer's "Vegetarianism" (*LBR* p. 603, manual p. 173) which is largely expository.

Jacob Alexander
Nitrite: Preservative or Carcinogen? (p. 593)

We think that Alexander produced an excellent research paper and that you may want to make considerable use of it if you require your students to write a research paper.

You may, for instance, want to ask a student to read the Abstract aloud in class, and then also to read aloud the first paragraph of the paper itself. What differences do the members of the class notice? The abstract is, to put it bluntly, quite a mouthful (the second sentence contains thirty-five words) and though it is interesting—how can a statement about cancer-causing agents in food not be interesting?—it is scarcely gripping. In our view, this colorlessness is *not* a fault. Abstracts, because they are essentially generalizations, inevitably lack the color or liveliness of the concrete details that make most writing readable.

By way of contrast, the first sentence of the paper itself contains almost as many words (thirty-two) as the second sentence of the abstract, yet is far more interesting. If you ask the class *why* this opening paragraph is more interesting, someone will surely point out that it contains an alarming (and therefore interesting) concrete detail: "average Americans eat their weight in food additives every year."

But even if you don't assign your students to write a research paper, you may want to ask them to read this essay, simply to think about its argument and its ways of arguing—i.e., you may want to assign it for the same reasons that you assign any other reading in *The Little, Brown Reader*.

Donna Maurer
Vegetarianism (p. 603)

To answer our first questions following the text ("How would you define vegetarianism? Do all vegetarians observe similar practices? If not, what is the range of vegetarian practices?") we offer here the following paragraphs from the entry on Vegetarianism by Donna Maurer from the *Encyclopedia of Food and Culture*.

Varieties of Vegetarianism
A wide range of dietary practices falls under the rubric of "vegetarianism." People who practice the strictest version, veganism, do not use any animal products or by-products. They do not eat meat, poultry, or seafood, nor do they wear leather or wool. They avoid foods that contain such animal by-products as whey and gelatin and do not use products that have been tested on animals.

Other vegetarians limit their avoidances to food. For example, ovo-lacto vegetarians consume eggs and dairy products but not meat, poultry, and seafood. Ovo vegetarians do not consume dairy products, and lacto vegetarians consume dairy products but not eggs. Semivegetarians occasionally consume some or all animal products and may or may not consider themselves vegetarians. Studies suggest that semivegetarians outnumber "true" vegetarians by about four to one.

These terms define the various types of vegetarians by what they do not consume. Consequently, many vegetarians are concerned that nonvegetarians view vegetarian diets as primarily prohibitive and restrictive. They emphasize that following a vegetarian diet often leads people to consume a wider variety of foods than many meat eaters do, as vegetarians often include a wider range of fruits, vegetables, grains, and legumes in their diets.

We then ask: "If you do not know the answers to these questions, what sources might you use to retrieve reliable explanations?" A few students might suggest the *Encyclopedia of Food and Culture*, but most will list the Web, which provides a useful opportunity to discuss (a) the reliability of sources found on the Net, and (b) how to document such sources. (Our search with Yahoo for "vegetarianism" produced 621,000 results in 11 seconds!)

Paul Goldberger
Quick! Before It Crumbles! (p. 606)

This short piece can be used effectively as an introduction to *analysis* or *comparison*. With a little help students can see how a comparison enables one to see more clearly the thing one is trying to understand. (Howard Nemerov astutely said, "If you want to understand something, look at something else.") Goldberger's first sentence contrasts the sugar wafer with "the ancient forms of traditional, individually baked cookies." That is, when one calls to mind a traditional cookie, one sees more clearly what is special about the sugar wafer. Note, also, that when Goldberger moves on in his next paragraph, to the Fig Newton, he begins with a comparison ("This, too, is a sandwich") and then moves to a contrast ("but different in every way from the Sugar Wafer").

Peter Singer
Animal Liberation (p. 609)

This essay is relatively long and closely reasoned, but we include it because it is lucid and on a subject of great interest to most students. Many of them are meat-eaters, and many perform experiments on animals in biology and psychology courses. This essay will not change many minds, but it will provoke responses. If an instructor has already taught a few of the shorter essays, students may well be ready to take on this relatively long one.

Singer knows that readers are likely to think animal liberation is a joke, so he begins where they are: the first paragraph reminds them that black liberation, gay liberation, and women's liberation all have required, and have brought about, an expansion of moral horizons. Only in the second paragraph does he get to animal liberation, and this paragraph chiefly introduces some names. The third paragraph summarizes the gist of the book he is reviewing, by quoting what Singer takes to be the central message. The fourth paragraph recognizes that the reader is likely to be skeptical, and Singer summarizes, fairly enough, an imagined reader's (and probably the real reader's) skepticism. The fifth paragraph traps the reader; the skeptical reply of the fourth paragraph is now shown to be inadequate. The sixth paragraph briefly and approvingly quotes Jeremy Bentham on equality, and though the quotation of course does not settle the matter, we now realize that there is an issue, and that the issue is not frivolous. The seventh paragraph quotes Bentham again, now directly on the subject of animal rights, and Singer insists, quite simply, "Surely Bentham was right." All this, we see in the next paragraph, is a way of bringing us to a position that we probably share with Singer: animals other than humans can suffer. In short, Singer is fully aware of the probable responses of his readers, and he takes these responses into account as he proceeds. Whether or not one agrees with Singer's argument, his way of proceeding surely is right and worthy of imitation.

We find Singer's arguments convincing, and we think it is evident that Singer is thoroughly sensible, for in his final paragraph he asks, "Can a purely moral demand of this kind succeed?" and he recognizes that "Animal Liberation will require greater altruism on the part of mankind than any other liberation movement, since animals are incapable of demanding it for themselves." We say that we find the argument convincing—yet we are not vegetarians, perhaps simply because of the force of old habits. We have not yet been moved by the necessary altruism—but perhaps when we next reread the essay.

A good deal has now been published about the rights (or absence of rights) of animals, much of it taking off from Singer's essay. Instructors who wish to give students practice in summarizing, analyzing, and evaluating may want to refer them to Michael Fox, "Animal Suffering and Animal Rights," *Ethics*, 88 (1978), which criticizes Singer, and to Singer's reply in the same volume, and to Fox's rejoinder, again in the same volume. For a rather crude response to Singer's position, see Timothy Noah's "Monkey Business," *The New Republic*, June 3, 1982. For a curiously perverse misunderstanding of Singer, see R. G. Frey, *Rights, Killing and Suffering* (1984). Frey claims to be directing his arguments against Singer, but he seems to think that if we can reduce or eliminate the pain or suffering of animals we have the moral right to kill them. Behind or beneath this view is Frey's view that "we cannot agree about the morality of taking human life so how likely are we to agree about the morality of taking animal life?" Far more thoughtful are Richard Ryder's *Victims of Science* (1983), a strong statement against the use of animals in research, and Andrew N. Rowen, *Of Mice, Models, and Men* (1984), a balanced view of this sort of research. Rowen finds that some medical advances can be attributed to research on animals, but he also argues that much research on animals is needlessly painful and often unproductive. Tom Regan's *All That Dwell Therein* (1982) is a collection of essays on various aspects of animal liberation; Regan's *The Case for Animal Rights* (1983) is an extended and sometimes puzzling philosophic argument on behalf of animals. Additional articles may be located in *The Philosopher's Index*, which gives abstracts.

Other selections in the text that pair well with "Animal Liberation": Anonymous, "Confessions of an Erstwhile Child" p. 151 and Swift, "A Modest Proposal" p. 621.

Topics for Critical Thinking and Writing

1. Suppose someone were to say to you, "The idea that animals have rights is absurd. After all, a dog does not have the right to vote." In a paragraph, reply to this argument.

2. Consider the following statement by a contemporary philosopher, William Frankena:

> All men are to be treated as equals, not because they are equal, in any respect, but simply because they are human. They are human because they have emotions and desires, and are able to think, and hence are capable of enjoying a good life in a sense in which other animals are not.
>
> —"The Concept of Social Justice," in R. Brandt, ed.,
> *Social Justice* (1962), p. 19

    How would Singer reply to Frankena's argument?

3. On May 15, 1976, *The New York Times* reported that a court acquitted Captain Cyril E. LaBrecque of manslaughter. His schooner had been wrecked, and he, his wife, his Labrador retriever, and one crewman took to the lifeboat. Three other crewmen could not fit into the lifeboat, but they hung on to it for almost ten hours, until two of them died from exposure in the icy Atlantic. At the trial it was asserted that in order to make room for one of the men clinging to the lifeboat, Captain LaBrecque tried to lift the eighty-pound dog out of the boat but could not, and that had he struggled with the dog the boat might have capsized. In your opinion, would Peter Singer argue that the dog had as much right to be in the lifeboat as any of the human beings? If on rereading Singer's essay you find evidence that, you believe, commits him to the view that the animal is not to be excluded, cite the evidence, summarizing and perhaps briefly quoting it. Similarly, if you find that Singer's arguments in "Animal Liberation" do not commit him to this view, point to the evidence. (Related question: Suppose the boat holds only four people, but five people are present. On what basis is one person excluded? Sex? Age? Intellectual ability? Strength? Or what?)

4. (This question requires the student to do research.) In paragraph 33 Singer refers to Ruth Harrison's essay "On Factory Farming," in *Animals, Men and Morals* (1972), edited by Stanley and Rosalind Godlovitch and John Harris. He also refers to Ruth Harrison's book *Animal Machines* (1964). If possible, look at these books or at Page Smith and Charles Daniel's *The Chicken Book* (1975), or at Michael Fox's *Farm Animals* (1984), or at the chapter titled "Down on the Factory Farm" in Singer's book *Animal Liberation* (1975). Even if the books are not available, you may be able to find out something about factory farming by reading some book reviews. You will learn, for instance, that five or six laying

hens are confined to a wire cage measuring 18 by 20 inches, and that a veal calf is confined to a stall 2 feet wide. (Reviews can be located through the *Book Review Index.*) You can also find out about factory farming by consulting the *Readers' Guide to Periodical Literature* or by consulting the Web. In any case, find some material on modern methods of chicken farming, and then write an essay of 500 to 700 words, sketching the system. Most of your essay will be a summary of material that you have read, but you may also want to use some brief quotations. Be sure to cite the sources of all quotations and also the sources that you summarize. (Instructors making this assignment can use passages in Singer's essay as examples of effective summaries, the use and form of quotations and of footnotes, and how to reduce the number of footnotes by citing sources within the body of the essay.)

Jonathan Swift
A Modest Proposal (p. 621)

Much of the voluminous writing on this short satire is devoted to Swift's use of a persona or mask, and especially to reconciling the persona with those passages in which we hear Swift's voice rather than the projector's. One desperate view, for example, holds that when the persona is apparently speaking out of character, the persona is really using irony and thus—though he is talking sense—he means the opposite of what he says. Our own view is different. We assume that when a satirist uses a persona he wants us at last to see through the mask, and once we have seen through the mask, we enjoy seeing the real face as well as the mask. That is, when we read the title and subtitle of Swift's essay, and even the first few paragraphs, we are at first taken in. But then we begin to suspect that what sounds matter of fact, for example, is cold-blooded or even crazy. And then we get the joke; we realize that we have been taken. We are reading a satire, we see a satirist at work, and there really is no reason why the satirist should consistently keep the mask in front of his face.

One place where we hear Swift's own voice is in the poke at England (paragraph 31): "I could name a country which would be glad to eat up our whole nation." But notice that the satire in this essay is not directed wholly toward England; Swift saves much of his fury for the Irish, especially in the two paragraphs preceding the one from which we have just quoted. In paragraph 29, after saying, "let no man talk to me of other expedients," Swift lists various proposals that he had seriously advocated in earlier writings and that were still available to the Irish, such as the use of locally manufactured clothing and furniture instead of imported goods and the development of habits of prudence and honesty. The object of the satire is Irish folly quite as much as English rapacity: the Irish have refused to take practical measures and have refused to cure "the expensiveness of pride, vanity, idleness, and gaming in our women," and so Swift now, in fury, tells them there is only one way left. The ironic contrast, then, is not merely between the barbaric solution the projector offers and the compassionate solution that the English should offer, but between one kind of Irish idiocy (the projector's) and another (that of the Irish themselves).

The most admired passages in which the projector speaks are these: the first paragraph, with its slightly crazy reference to "three, four, or six children"; the second paragraph, especially its latter half, in view of what we later learn about how this "preserver of the nation" hopes that children can be made into "useful members of the commonwealth"; the fourth paragraph, with its reference to "a child just dropped from its dam" (the projector thinks of human beings as beasts); the sixth paragraph (beginning "The number of souls"), with its cool mathematical calculations, treating human beings as mere units; the reference (paragraph 14) to the cost of nursing a beggar's child, "about 2s. per annum, rags included"; the reference (paragraph 19) to dying "as fast as can be reasonably expected"; and the final paragraph.

Topics for Critical Thinking and Writing

1. Write your own "Modest Proposal," using some of Swift's strategies, exposing a topic of your own choice. Choose a serious topic (for instance, racism, anti-Semitism, environmental pollution, unemployment), and offer a solution that is outrageous but developed with relentless logic. Your essay should be about 1,000 words long.

2. Swift's proposal is, in large measure, built on taking a metaphor literally: landlords devour the Irish poor. Take a metaphor (for example, "certain people should be put in their place," or "it's a dog-eat-dog world") and set forth a modest proposal (500 words) in which you take the metaphor literally.

Jimmy Carter
My Boyhood Home (p. 628)

To answer our second question in the text: President Carter's recollections "deserve little fondness," we suppose, because they are a record of very hard work and many hardships. The Carter family lived in rural Georgia during the Depression. They had no running water, central heat, indoor toilets, or electricity. But evidence of fondness abounds. President Carter's descriptions of their house and land, their work, and their family life suggest pride and love. Even the poorest of our students live now with more physical comfort and in greater affluence than the Carters. But roughly fifty percent of our students live in broken homes, as children or as parents. Instead of images of Daddy reading newspapers and magazines and Mama reading books, what is it our students remember about their early years at home? Visits with an estranged parent? Stepparents? Nursery schools or nannies? Coming home from school to an empty apartment? Students are, for the most part, unwilling to talk about the divorce of their parents or to write about it. But if you ask them why Carter remembers his childhood fondly, the closeness of the Carter family will almost surely surface.

One can look at the passage in which President Carter remembers the family listening to the radio together and names their favorite programs. One can ask: Was listening to the radio or watching TV together habitual in your family? Or did you listen and watch separately? An essay topic might be based on a comparison of the Carter family with a family the student knows well—it may or may not be his or her own family, it might be a "typical" family in the time and place of the student's childhood.

In recounting the radio broadcast of the Joe Louis/Max Schmeling fight, President Carter reveals the customs and mores of a segregated society.

Topic for Critical Thinking and Writing

In roughly 500 words, describe the first place you remember living in. From your description, your readers should be able to infer something of the life of your family there and your attitudes toward the place, then and now.

Jane Jacobs
A Good Neighborhood (p. 635)

This selection nicely illustrates illustration; to explain what she means by "a good city street neighborhood," Jacobs focuses on "the stores where people leave keys for their friends." She then gives us half a page about Joe Cornacchia, a paragraph about several other custodians (or rather about their shops), and then a page about Bernie Jaffe. By the time we finish the essay we are convinced that we know the sort of neighborhood she is talking about. She might, of course, have conveyed the sense of a neighborhood by talking about the way adults respond to the street games the children play or the relationship between the residents and the cops. The point: she has helped us to understand a "good" neighborhood by giving illustrations that support the diagnosis.

Topic for Critical Thinking and Writing

In the first two paragraphs Jacobs defines "a good city street neighborhood." Using her standards, describe, analyze, and evaluate a college dormitory or any neighborhood you have lived in and know well.

E. B. White
The Door (p. 638)

The hero of this enduring fable about the assaults of progress on the psyche finds himself, on a visit to "the city," in a model house exhibiting unconventional arrangements of space (no walls) and furniture of extruded plastic with pseudoscientific names. His ensuing disorientation reminds him of a psychologist's experiment with rats who were trained to jump at cards that collapsed to allow the rats to be rewarded by food. The cards were then changed so that the psychologist might study the rats being frustrated into insanity. The man reflects on four "doors" he had once trusted, but found illusory: religion ("the long sweet words with the holy sound"), science ("the equation . . . and the picture of the amoeba"), economic security (the check), and love, in which he still yearns to believe (the picture of the girl). He thinks also of two men similarly frustrated: the man in Jersey who rebelled with a heroic but insane act of destruction, and the poet who died, exhausted from pursuing his ideals. Our hero is briefly tempted by a prefrontal lobotomy, a scientific alternative to insanity, or death. But instead, he cautiously finds his way out of the house, down the escalator, and back into natural light, among other people, and on solid ground.

William R. Steinhoff, in the December 1961 issue of *College English*, discloses many of White's sources for "The Door." The "central analogy" of the story, some of the language, and perhaps the title come from a report in *Life* (March 6, 1939) of an experiment on rats conducted by Professor Norman Maier. At about the same time, *The New York Times* covered an exhibit at Rockefeller Center of model homes and furnishings, which included a washable house and a plastic-coated piano. The man in Jersey, a 68-year-old inventor, lost a fortune in a divorce settlement and then went berserk when Boss Hague appointed Frank Hague Jr. to the New Jersey Court of Errors and Appeals. "My friend the poet" was Don Marquis, about whom White had written movingly in an introduction to *Archy and Mehitabel* (1931). And finally, *The Times*, also in March 1939, had described the relatively new technique of prefrontal lobotomy as "an operation for correcting the disease of civilization."

James Wright
Lying in a Hammock at William Duffy's Farm
in Pine Island, Minnesota (p. 642)

It seems to us that the title is somewhat paradoxical, in its implication of utter relaxation and apartness—lying *in* a hammock, *at* someone's farm, *in* an island—and (on the other hand) the almost pedantic or fussy specification of the locale. And we find the rest of the poem paradoxical too.

The speaker's eye ranges. He takes in the view above (a natural starting place for someone lying in a hammock), then looks "Down the ravine," then "To my right," and then, at the end, up again ("I lean back"), when he observes the chicken hawk. In a sense he ends where he began, but meanwhile he has explored (or at least surveyed) a good deal. He has, from his sleep-like condition in the hammock, begun by seeing a bronze-colored butterfly "Asleep," then has heard the distant cowbells, and has seen "The droppings of last year's horses" (so we get some extension into time as well as into space), and then glances again at the sky. This exploration—all from the hammock—is marked by keen yet imaginative observations.

Let's go back a moment, to the first perception, the "bronze butterfly / Asleep." The poet is describing the color, but the effect is paradoxical, giving the reader a fragile insect made of an enduring material. From perceptions of colors ("bronze," "black," "green") we go to aural perceptions ("The cowbells follow one another") and then back to visual perceptions (the horse droppings, now "golden stones"). In all of this beauty there is a keen sense of isolation—the cows and horses are not present, and even the chicken hawk is looking for home. Now, "as the evening darkens," the speaker has an epiphany, uttered in the final line.

The final line probably comes to the reader as a shock, and perhaps the reader is uncertain about how to take it. Is the speaker kidding? Or is he saying, in dead seriousness, all creatures except me seem to have their place in a marvelously beautiful, peaceful nature, whereas I am not even in my own home? Our own impression is that, whatever he says, *we* feel that he has not wasted his life, since he has so interestingly recorded his perceptions.

For further study of Wright, see *Collected Prose*, ed. Anne Wright (1983), and *Above the River: The Complete Poems*, with an introduction by Donald Hall (1990). The best critical discussions can be found in *The Pure Clear Word: Essays on the Poetry of James Wright*, ed. Dave Smith (1982). Also recommended: Kevin Stein, *James Wright: The Poetry of a Grown Man* (1989), and Andrew Elkins, *The Poetry of James Wright* (1991).

13

BODY AND SOUL

Illustrations

Henri Cartier-Bresson
Place de l'Europe, Paris, 1932 (p. 646)

In our discussion of writing about pictures (p. 106) we use a quotation of Cartier-Bresson as an epigraph:

> I am after the one unique picture whose composition possesses such vigor and richness, and whose content so radiates outwards from it, that this single picture is a whole story in itself.

Almost all of Cartier-Bresson's comments about photography are variations of this point. Several collections of his photographs include prefaces by Cartier-Bresson. Some of his remarks are collected in *Photographers on Photography* (1966), ed. Nathan Lyons, and in *Dialogue with Photography* (1979), eds. Paul Hill and Thomas Cooper. One example, from *Dialogue with Photography*, is Cartier-Bresson's quotation from Victor Hugo: "Form is the essence brought to the surface." This quotation, like the epigraph, provides a good entry into his pictures.

This picture, also known as *Behind St. Lazare*, is almost unbelievable in its perfection. The man leaping over the puddle is predictably imaged in the puddle, but who could have predicted that he would be echoed by the leaping dancer on the poster, or that the curve of the dancer's back and elevated leg would be echoed by the hoops in the water? Of course, when one starts looking for a pattern, one usually finds it, but we don't think we are going too far in saying that even the hands on the clock tower seem to echo the man's posture and contribute to the pattern, and that the angles formed by the man's legs and the reflection of his legs are echoed in the angles of the buildings. But perhaps we are going a bit too far when we say that, in the ladder and the pentagon formed by the man's legs and their reflection, we see (almost) an arrow pointing in the direction in which the man is leaping, and this arrow is a giant version of the palings in the fence.

Ken Gray
Lifted Lotus (p. 647)

The picture comes from a book on yoga for two, Cain Carroll and Lori Kimata's *Partner Yoga* (2000). The first thing we should say is that although we have read this book (and others) and have taken an occasional course in yoga, we know very little about yoga, and it is likely that many composition instructors and their students are far more adept and more knowledgeable than we are. The second thing we should say is that in the United States, and indeed in the West in general, yoga almost always is the school called hatha yoga, which is very different from what yoga means to most Hindus.

The word *yoga* derives from a Sanskrit word for union, or joining or yoking; *join* and *yoke* both come from this same root. Yoga seeks to free the individual from ordinary awareness (life in Plato's cave, perhaps) and to join or yoke the individual's consciousness to its spiritual source, to god or God. Hatha yoga (*hatha* is variously said to mean *exertion, force,* and *sun-moon*) is largely concerned with physical postures (*asanas*) and breathing exercises (*pranayama*) in order to achieve control over the body. That is, hatha yoga (as we understand it) is a program of physical culture, pursued in order to coordinate forces in the body. In India, such procedures are merely a preparatory discipline for traditional yoga, joining—by means of meditation techniques—the individual to a greater spiritual force.

What of the photograph that we reproduce? It comes, as we have said, from a book called *Partner Yoga,* where it is accompanied by a warning: "This pose is recommended only for advanced yogis or those who can successfully perform all of the other partner lifts" (p. 164). Further, it warns that when learning this posture, "It is a good idea to have a third person present to serve as a spotter. The spotter can support the lifted partner if she needs to adjust her position and/or help prevent a dangerous fall" (p. 165). A few other quotations from the book will give you an idea of what is going on—and its distance from classic yoga. In a section called "Benefits," the authors write (p. 165):

Partner One
    Strengthens the thighs, hips, and abdominal muscles • Gives a much deserved break to veins in the legs and feet, relieving, and possibly preventing, varicose veins • Heightens awareness of balance and weight distribution • Brings the mind into a single pointed focus (Advanced yogis, this is the perfect opportunity to practice the sixth limb of yoga, *dharana*) • Intensely heightens awareness of the feet, legs, and hips

Partner Two
    Gives an opportunity to closely examine fear and trust.

(If this discussion of "benefits" is accurate, in yoga as in much of the rest of life, men get the best deals.) The reference to *dharana* is indeed a reference to classic yoga, which speaks of *eight-limbed yoga*, techniques to bring the practitioner out of ordinary awareness and into a state of consciousness that is achieved by union with a higher spiritual power. *Dharana*, the sixth of the eight stages, is a kind of concentration that is said to be a prerequisite for deep meditation. The first five "limbs" are said to be preparatory or "external"; the last three are said to be crucial or "internal," so *dharana*, the first of the final three, is the beginning of the end.

A few words about the lotus position (Sanskrit: *padmasana*), in which the woman in our photo sits. It involves sitting cross-legged, each foot resting on the opposite thigh. The back is erect, and the hands are in a specified gesture or *mudra*. (More about the *mudra* in a moment.) In Hindu thinking, the lotus (a plant of the water lily family) is a symbol of the centers of consciousness in the body, and the fact that the flower floats on the water yet remains dry is interpreted as symbolic of the spiritual aspirant who lives in this world but is not sullied by it. Somewhat similarly, in Buddhism the lotus is a symbol of truth, flourishing above the mud in which it is rooted. Now for the *mudra:* in this instance the mudra is called *namo anjalikarmamudra*, "prayer." The hands are joined vertically at the level of the breast, palm against palm, fingers against fingers. More precisely, since the man's thumbs seem to be overlapping, he may be making a slightly different but closely related mudra. In any case, the gestures signify worship, adoration. E. Dale Saunders in a fascinating book, *Mudra: A Study of Symbolic Gesture in Japanese Buddhist Sculpture* (1960), suggests that this gesture "may derive from Hindu etiquette, in which it is a gesture of offering, of adoration, and of salutation" (p. 77).

Short Views

We have never had any difficulty in discussing religious matters in the college classroom, but we do know that some of our colleagues prefer to avoid talking about religion. Plenty of things in this chapter can be discussed without getting into matters of religion.

Among the Short Views, for instance, one can take the second, Napoleon's "Anatomy is destiny." Ask students to paraphrase the sentence and to offer supporting evidence for its validity. Almost surely someone will mention the Napoleonic complex, the idea that some short men compensate for their minimal stature by aggressive or grandiose behavior, i.e., Napoleon's own anatomy (they may say) determined his destiny. And, come to think of it, perhaps Napoleon's most famous comment is, "An army marches on its stomach," which suggests that when push comes to shove, biology, not a lofty ideal, is what motivates the soldier.

Anonymous
Muddy Road (p. 650)

We use this story in *An Introduction to Literature*, 14th ed. (2006), where we discuss it in terms of plot and character. Although in an introductory course in composition the story will probably be taught chiefly in terms of theme, rather than in terms of the structure of the fiction, we nevertheless suggest that you may want to talk about it in terms of story-telling. The following comment is drawn from our *Introduction*.

The opening paragraph, though simple and matter-of-fact, holds our attention because we sense that something interesting is going to happen during the journey along a muddy road on a rainy day. Perhaps we even sense, somehow, by virtue of the references to the mud and the rain, that the journey itself rather than the travelers' destination will be the heart of the story: getting there will be more than half the fun. And then, after the introduction of the two characters and the setting, we quickly get a complication, the encounter with the girl. Still, there is apparently no conflict, though in "Ekido did not speak again until that night" we sense an unspoken conflict, an action (or, in this case, an inaction) that must be explained, an unbalance that must be righted before we finish. At last Ekido, no longer able to contain his thoughts, lets his indignation burst out: "We monks don't go near females, especially not young and lovely ones. It is dangerous. Why did you do that?"

His statement and his question reveal not only his moral principles but also his insecurity and the anger that grows from it. More specifically, of course, it indicates the gap between his spiritual ideals and his fleshly thoughts. And now, when the conflict is out in the open, comes the brief reply that reveals Tanzan's very different character, very different spiritual condition. The reply, which we could not have predicted, strikes us as exactly right, bringing the story to a perfect end, i.e., to a point (like the ends of Jesus's parables) at which there is no more to be said.

We have sometimes taught this story *without* having assigned it. We begin reading the anecdote aloud, stopping after "A heavy rain was still falling." We then ask, "What do you think will happen now?" Someone is bound to volunteer, "They will meet someone." Whom will they meet? (It may be necessary to remind the students that Tanzan and Ekido are two men.) You will certainly be informed that if two men meet someone, the someone will be a woman. Continue reading, "Coming around a bend, they met a lovely girl." After "unable to cross the intersection," ask again what will happen, and entertain answers until you get an appropriate response. Read again, and pause after "Why did you do that?" Now tell the class that the story has one more line of print, and ask them to supply possible endings. After a few suggestions, read the final line. The students will see the perfect rightness of the anecdote.

D. T. Suzuki
What Is Zen? (p. 650)

As Buddhism spread from India to Central Asia, Tibet, China, and Japan, it took many forms; the form most widely known in the West is what the Chinese call Chan (from the Sanskrit *dhyana*, "meditation") and the Japanese call Zen. Buddhism seems to have entered China late in the first century A.D., but it apparently did not flourish until the fourth century, and Chan did not become a distinctive sect before the sixth century. Chan—or Zen, to use the more familiar term—itself developed two schools: one school advocated "gradual enlightenment," usually achieved by sitting meditation (Japanese: *zazen*), whereas the other subscribed to "sudden enlightenment," which might come at any moment, for example, when the master made a gesture or while one was chopping wood. (It should be understood that sudden enlightenment might come only after long years of meditation, and so the achievement of enlightenment in this way might take longer than the achievement of gradual enlightenment.)

Although one aspect of Zen thinking minimizes the study of texts, Zen nevertheless is much interested in certain Buddhist texts, and it has produced a vast body of commentary. One of the most studied books is the *Lakavatara Sutra* (first century A.D.). Here are two passages from this sutra (Buddhist scripture) that are widely described as providing a philosophic basis for Zen:

Things are understood in their true essence when intellect reaches its limit, and its processes . . . are transcended by a higher faculty. Intuition is such a faculty, linking the intellectual mind with the universal mind.

Some think they can achieve the goal of tranquility by suppressing mental activity. This is a mistake. . . . The goal of tranquility is reached not by suppressing all mental activity but by freeing oneself from discriminations and attachments.

There is always a certain irony (or at least paradox) inherent in writings that denigrate writing, but Suzuki manages to escape ridicule, partly, no doubt, because he tells engaging stories. However skeptical readers may be about Zen wisdom, they can scarcely be unimpressed by the stories.

In our biographical note on Suzuki, we try to define *satori*, "enlightenment" or "awakening," pointing out that "The awakening is from a world of blind strivings (including those of reason and of morality); the awakened being, free from a sense of the self in opposition to all other things, perceives the unity of all things." Students who have seen *Star Wars* may remember hearing (and cheering) the advice, "Use the Force, Luke. Let go."

Topics for Critical Thinking and Writing

1. Suzuki tells two illustrative stories or parables, one of a priest and one of a swordsman. Make up a third story to illustrate the nature of enlightenment. Or make up a story to illustrate the nature of religious faith, or of charity.

2. What relevance does Zen have to secular life, for instance, to education, or to a sport or skill? Some instructors may want to make use—in the classroom or on the court—of W. Timothy Gallwey's *The Inner Game of Tennis* (2000). This how-to-do-it book includes a few Zen stories and is said to have raised the level of tennis playing.

Langston Hughes
Salvation (p. 654)

Hughes, of course, is writing as an adult, but the simplicity of many of his sentences ("But not really saved. It happened like this") and of much of his diction ("There was a big revival") is appropriate to a boy not yet thirteen. This is not really the speech of a youngster ("escorted" in the first paragraph, "dire" in the third, "work-gnarled" in the fourth), but on the whole the style evokes the child's state of mind; we might say that we are chiefly conscious of the youthful subject rather than of the mature writer. But a very artful and adult ironic writing pervades the piece. Notice, for instance, the deflating effect that the last, brief sentence of paragraph 3 has upon the slightly longer previous sentence: "And some of them jumped up and went to Jesus right away. But most of us just sat there." And, of course, the contrast between the hypocritical, grinning Westley (who surely did not cry that night) and the narrator effectively emphasizes Hughes's sense of isolation. If the story is, on the surface, amusing, it is also finally serious and moving.

Henry David Thoreau
Economy (p. 657)

We have taught this selection often, and in a variety of ways, and usually through a paper assignment that the students work on before the first class meeting.

Once, we asked the students to focus on the opening sentence—"The mass of men lead lives of quiet desperation"—and to explain, with evidence drawn from the text, how Thoreau seeks to prove this assertion. Does he make a convincing case or not?

On another occasion, we featured the opening sentence and asked the students to work from their own experiences and observations: "From what you have seen and heard, do you believe that, as Thoreau contends, most people 'lead lives of quiet desperation'?"

This second assignment led to uneven results. Some of the students wrote thoughtfully in response to Thoreau's claim, but others had trouble and struggled their way through a series of large generalizations. If we give this assignment again, we likely will make it more precise.

Even a slight adjustment or two might help: "From your conversations with classmates and interactions with them, would you say that most of them 'lead lives of quiet desperation'?"

Maybe hone the assignment even more: "From your conversations with classmates and interactions with them, would you say that most of them 'lead lives of quiet desperation'? What sorts of things have they said, and what kinds of things have they done, that have led you to conclude that Thoreau is right, or else that he is wrong?"

It's important to prompt the students to consider the specific meanings of the words in this sentence. Here are definitions from the excellent *American Heritage Dictionary*, fourth edition (2000).

Mass:
1. A unified body of matter with no specific shape: *a mass of clay.*
2. A grouping of individual parts or elements that compose a unified body of unspecified size or quantity: *"Take mankind in mass, and for the most part, they seem a mob of unnecessary duplicates"* (Herman Melville).

3. A large but nonspecific amount or number: *a mass of bruises.*
4. The principal part; the majority: *the mass of the continent.*
5. The physical volume or bulk of a solid body.

Quiet:
1. Making no noise; silent: *a quiet audience at the concert.*
2. Free of noise; hushed: *a quiet place for studying.*
3. Calm and unmoving; still: *floating on quiet waters.*
4. Free of turmoil and agitation; untroubled. See synonyms at still.
5. Restful; soothing: *a quiet afternoon nap; a warm, quiet bath.*
6. Tranquil; serene: *a quiet manner.*
7. Not showy or garish; restrained: *a room decorated in quiet colors.*

Desperation:
1. The condition of being desperate. See synonyms at despair.
2. Recklessness arising from despair.

Desperate:
1. Having lost all hope; despairing.
2. Marked by, arising from, or showing despair: *the desperate look of hunger; a desperate cry for help.*
3. Reckless or violent because of despair: *a desperate criminal.*
4. Undertaken out of extreme urgency or as a last resort: *a desperate attempt to save the family business.*

These definitions are pertinent to the kind of assertion that Thoreau makes. No, that is not quite right: these words, with these meanings and associations, *constitute* the assertion that Thoreau makes. He uses the word "mass," for example, precisely for its sense of a bulky, awkward lack of specificity; most men are globbed together, not individualized at all, because of the desperation they share about the lives they lead but feel unable or unwilling to change.

For the papers to be good, the students need to have a feeling for the words they are responding to. You might consider lingering over Thoreau's "men" as well. We may assume that by "men" he meant women as well as men. But maybe he did not; he may have been directing his arguments in this essay very much at men, not at women. Does it make a difference to our response if we interpret men to mean "men" or "men and women"? Do Thoreau's words apply today to men more than women, or to both equally?

We have lingered a bit over this sentence because it indicates the approach we favor to this selection. We key a writing assignment to a claim or assertion, aiming (as we have learned through experience to do) to give the response to Thoreau some precision and making sure that the students actually see and hear their way *into* the meanings of the words that Thoreau uses in this statement or that one.

This selection as a whole, from beginning to end, is a stimulating, provocative one. But many students have told us that they find Thoreau hectoring and tedious. And we concede that there are grounds for these complaints. *Walden* has many striking passages, but it does go on and on. To adapt Samuel Johnson's remark about *Paradise Lost,* no one has wished *Walden* longer than it is. So we are inclined to suggest that you perceive this selection from "Economy" as valuable for its local rewards—a pointed and suggestive sentence, an artfully organized paragraph. With Thoreau's writings, success in the classroom and in papers is frequently a matter of choosing your spots, of focusing the students' attention on pieces of the text that they can manage a response to.

The next time we teach this Thoreau selection, we are inclined to try a classroom experiment. We'll ask each student to select the most important sentence in it, the one that expresses most vividly the core of Thoreau's message. Maybe we will make this a writing assignment that the students undertake beforehand—that is a good way to guarantee that the students come to class prepared with something to say. But we might simply make this a reading assignment: make your choice of sentence and come to class ready to argue for your choice.

We expect that the choice of sentences will vary quite a bit and that the range of sentences will move us around the selection. We hope, too, that the students will feel some debate in the air, as each one makes his or her case for why *this* sentence, rather than that one, is the most important one.

We might also get a good writing assignment from this activity after the discussion is done: "OK, we have nominated a number of sentences as candidates for the 'most important.' Do you still believe that your choice is the best, or, now that you have heard what others have said, would you make a different choice?"

If we're lucky, we'll get some good essays from this assignment. But in a way it is not crucial that we do. The value of this kind of assignment is that it impels the students to reflect upon the discussion they have been part of— give some thought to it, that is, after the class is over. They came to class with a choice of a sentence, with a position. Others spoke on behalf of their choices and presented their arguments. Now, how does each student weigh and appraise his or her choice, his or her argument, alongside what others have said?

From time to time, it's not a bad idea to devise strategies that require students to pay sharp attention to what's taking place in the classroom. You might tell them what the "after-this-class-is-over" writing assignment will be *before* the discussion and debate occur. Or, if you are feeling a little devilish, you might not. If they haven't been paying close attention this time, this assignment might spur them to do so in the future!

Natalie Angier
The Sandbox: Bully for You:
Why Push Comes to Shove (p. 668)

We're interested in Angier's "The Sandbox" for several reasons. She writes about a topic that has been of great interest in the past few years. Her style is vigorous and she is always clever, often witty. Our students are keenly aware of bullying in schools, and they write well about it. And Angier appends one of the most famous and appealing ads ever published, for Charles Atlas's "Dynamic Tension."

The topic of bullies has been prominent because of the series of crimes committed by high school students, notably at Columbine and Santana High Schools. But Angier, while mentioning these events, also summarizes recent research on bullies, more thoroughly than most journalists. As for her style, her opening sentence is characteristically clever: "Some people are just fair game for being picked on and put down: lawyers, politicians, journalists, mothers-in-law and, now, bullies." She seems at first to be aggrieved for the victims—people who are "picked on and put down." But she is, of course, being ironic, as her list of victims demonstrates. And her language is ironic as well. The words "picked on and put down" and "ganging up on" suggest the activities of bullies, but she turns them around to have them suggest the activities *against* bullies. In her sixth paragraph she asserts that "legislators are struggling to beat each other to the punch in demanding that schools stamp out bad behavior," in language that continues to suggest aggression but now attributes it not to bullies but to legislators.

Is she treating a serious problem too lightly? We don't think so. She refers to Philip C. Rodkin, an assistant professor of educational psychology at the University of Illinois, who "pointed out that, despite all the attention being paid to the subject, the root causes of bullying remain a mystery." And she refers to other researchers who claim that "the incidence of serious bullying has very likely declined over the years." Another researcher, Frans de Waal, a primatologist, has observed that bullies need to be studied along with scape-goats, and some researchers have observed that "children in groups will often encourage, or at least not discourage, a bully's nasty acts against an under-ling." Moreover, "many bullies in fact are quite popular." In short, we don't think that Angier's humor denigrates the seriousness of the problem. Her article allows us to see that the problem exists, perhaps it has always existed, and, although it is being seriously studied, it remains a mystery.

Angier concludes her essay by referring to bullying behavior among adults, in business, for example, and how our attitudes toward this kind of bul-lying are ambivalent. J. P. Morgan was "a beefy, red-faced thick-necked finan-cial bully" (according to Robert M. LaFollette), but he was also "described by officials at Harvard University as a 'prince among merchants,'" "a man of 'skill, wisdom and courage.'" And in her last paragraph Angier refers to those in the international community who see America as "the biggest bully of them all." Had she written this article after September 11, 2001 (instead of in May 2001), would she have concluded it thus? And would she have alluded to Mayor Rudy Guilliani in her second paragraph? What do your students think?

Topic for Critical Thinking and Writing

In two or three paragraphs, describe some bullies you have known. Were they, in your opinion, unpopular or misfits? Or did you and your friends find them likeable, attractive, cool?

Robert Santos
My Men (p. 673)

This is a vivid, intense selection, and we have had success with it in the classroom. Students find Santos's descriptions to be absorbing, and also his reflections upon his experiences (e.g., paragraph 16, which begins, "I think it's funny how you can rationalize everything while you're there").

The lengthy paragraph 11 makes a nice choice to focus on. The short, staccato sentences; the sound effects; the movement back and forth from action to dialogue: we always read this paragraph aloud and invite students to explain why the writing here is compelling.

There is another purpose, however, that we hope to achieve through this selection. After we have discussed it for a while, and have highlighted both the descriptive and reflective moments in it and the language that Santos uses. . . . Well, we then remind the class of a fact that the *kind* of approach we have taken to the selection tends to make all of us forget—that it's an example of an oral history. In other words, we have to imagine this selection as "something that Santos said." It affects us as something spoken, rather than as something written.

You can guess where we are headed—to an exploration with the class of the issue of "voice" in writing. What we seek to articulate, for the students, is the challenge—and it is an interesting challenge—of creating a "personal voice" in their own prose.

All of us have been told: "Develop your own voice in your writing." "Sound like yourself and not like someone else." These are injunctions that we feature in the classroom and that authors of books on composition, style, and rhetoric emphasize.

Up to a point this is excellent advice. Indeed, we find it is helpful for students to keep in mind, while they revise, the questions, "How does this sound when I read it aloud?" and "Does this sound like me?" We joke with the class that everyone needs to start mumbling to their computer screen—that it's a good idea to read aloud the phrases and sentences that the student has written, all the more so since in the computer era it's fairly easy for us to produce a lot of prose. Writer's block is, nowadays, less of a problem than editor's block: students need to be helped to *hear* and *see* what needs to be done to make the prose on the screen cogent and coherent as a written essay when it becomes black print on pages of paper.

But our advice about "sounding like yourself" can only be taken so far. After all, an essay that a student prepares for her writing course isn't the same as the account of the essay she might give to her teacher during a conference—or that she might grumble about to a friend in the dorm. Of course it's true that all of us in a sense *edit* our speech—and often we wish we had edited it more carefully! But the editing of a written essay is a more deliberative, slower-paced matter. That's why we advise students to "revise carefully" and to "put a lot of time into the revision." Writing, as every writer knows, is rewriting.

It's not the easiest advice for a student to respond to, but we like to stress: "Work to make the essay sound like yourself, but remember too that you'll want to sound *better* than that in your prose." The voice we use in conversation isn't the voice we use in writing: we write in complete sentences and in organized paragraphs, with a defined beginning, middle, and end.

Students thus can do something valuable for their writing when they ask, "Does this really sound like me?" But they should be encouraged to perceive this advice as one part of the whole—that they are conveying to readers the sense, the feeling, of a voice, but are doing so through acts of writing and revision. Write, listen to what you have written, and now rewrite: the process goes something like that.

Rogelio R. Gomez
Foul Shots (p. 678)

Gomez's essay could have taken a different direction, and it is all the more valuable for our work in essay-writing courses because it did not. He could have focused on a painful memory and explained how he has now successfully moved beyond it. But instead he stresses that the pain lingers, even though two decades have passed. There's a tension, an anger and bitterness, in this selection that gives us charged feelings to delve into.

We begin with basic questions: What happened on that day when Gomez and his teammates traveled to Winston Churchill High? What was Gomez thinking and feeling then? What was the boys' response to the tossing of the bag of Fritos?

Once these basics have been established, we make our questions more provocative. For example: When the white boys tossed the bag of Fritos, do you think they meant to be cruel? Could someone say, Look, maybe this was insensitive, but really it was just a dumb prank? Why make such a big deal of something so minor? Gomez is now a well-educated, accomplished, and successful person—why is he drawn back to this episode of so long ago?

As we raise these questions and develop the discussion, we're trying to dramatize for students how something small-seeming can carry with it big and enduring meanings. The bag of Fritos, in itself, is trivial. What matters, of course, is that it symbolizes so much ("The bag seemed to grow before our eyes like a monstrous symbol of inferiority"). A symbol can be powerful and acquire a complex history: it can possess a life of its own. One is reminded here of the handkerchief that Iago uses to destroy the marriage of Othello and Desdemona, and of the leaf of grass that Whitman explores in his 1855 book *Leaves of Grass*.

We do something else with Gomez's essay. Nearly always during class discussion, someone says: "He needs to put the whole thing behind him," and "He should try to get over it." If by chance these comments are not made, we finesse them into the discussion ourselves, and the students readily accept them as appropriate kinds of remarks even if they disagree about applying them to Gomez. As teachers of writing and critical thinking, our interest is in prompting students to *think about and through* phrases and sentences like these. What does it mean to say, "I need to put the experience behind me?" How might we visualize such a statement? Does it really make sense? Is it something we can actually do? Does this advice sound good but prove impossible to put into practice? Furthermore, how *do* we get over something? What does it mean to say *that*, and how do we go about doing *that*?

In a writing course, we hope among other things to give students an interior feeling for language, a greater self-consciousness about it, so that they are more aware of the meanings and implications of their uses of language in speech as well as in writing. And we've found that the discussion of Gomez's essay provides us with opportunities for highlighting this skill, this relationship to language.

We admire the vigor and thrust of Gomez's prose—the action of his verbs (e.g., "snickering and laughing" and "mocking," in the first sentence alone), and the vivid metaphors and similes ("The evidence wrapped itself around our collective psyche like a noose"). But sometimes we feel that Gomez is too heavy with adjectives and adverbs, and that perhaps his essay might gain if his phrasing were cleaner, if he allowed his nouns and verbs to do the work.

"Smug smile," "smiled sardonically," "shiny new cars," "burning sense of inferiority," "glamorized models," "starkly contrasted," "shiny linoleum floor," "deft comment": we move through the essay, pausing over these phrases and asking the class in each instance, What does this adjective or adverb *do*, what does it contribute to the phrase that Gomez needs? Could the verb or the noun carry the meaning alone? How much, how little, does the extra word matter?

Hemingway had a point when he said that good writing is above all a matter of nouns and verbs, and this is especially true for students at an introductory level. Many of them are quick with adverbs and adjectives, which they use automatically. It's good for students to slow down and consider what they are doing and why. And it won't hurt to quote Mark Twain, from *Pudd'nhead Wilson:* "As to the adjective, when in doubt, strike it out."

Plato
Crito (p. 681)

We include Plato's "The Myth of the Cave" in our section "Teaching and Learning"; "Crito" might well be there too because it admirably shows the process of education. We try to indicate (manual, p. 89) some of the relationships between the form of a philosophic dialogue and a way of finding the truth.

Although this dialogue is not so central to Platonic philosophy as "The Myth of the Cave," it is unexcelled as a depiction of the philosopher living according to his principles. Socrates is loyal to the laws of Athens, a loyalty higher than that due to friends and family. His loyalty to the law is consistent with his principle that one must follow reason, not the opinion of the multitude; and reason unconditionally prohibits us from returning evil for evil. (In this connection we meet the famous analogy of the philosopher as a sort of athletic coach: just as the body must be governed by a specialist, so the soul, which lives on the good, must be governed not by the opinions of the multitude but by the knowledgeable man.) The good is a binding force, not dependent on how other people behave. But this means that the upholder of the good as an absolute must expect, in this world of the relative, to find himself in conflict.

A few words about the laws: The passage in which the laws are personified adds an emotional and somewhat mystical touch, thereby conveying the suggestion that, though the laws explicitly offer reasons, reasoning is not all that is involved. It is almost as though for a moment Socrates is lifted into heaven, where he utters his allegiance to heavenly principles, all the while talking easily and informally. The laws are the community's perception of the nature of things, i.e., of the Platonic ideas. In the laws the state sets forth, so far as it can, its understanding of the good; the laws are, for the individual, the earthly representatives of the good. Socrates shows Crito that the laws are not merely an individual's will. (The dialogue does *not* raise the possibility that the laws themselves may fail to conform to the idea of the good, and that the individual then has a right to resist them. The question raised is this: May an individual resist a lawful, though unfair, decision of the court?)

What of the end of the dialogue? Romano Guardini, in *The Death of Socrates* (1948, pp. 89–90), has a useful comment:

> Death is overcome by the spiritually awakening man's becoming aware of an absolute which stands on the other side of life's stream and its rhythms . . . ; by

his becoming aware of the Just, the True, the Holy or Good. In its presence he experiences a peculiar obligation, proceeding from the nature of validity itself—but also necessarily connected with this, something ultimate inside himself which has the faculty of responding to that validity and being bound by it: conscience.

Topic for Critical Thinking and Writing

Under what circumstances can you imagine yourself breaking a law in good conscience?

Robert Frost
Design (p. 693)

On Frost's "Design," see Randall Jarrell, *Poetry and the Age* (1953); Richard Poirier, *Robert Frost* (1977); Reuben A. Brower, *The Poetry of Robert Frost* (1963); Richard Ohmann, *College English* 28 (February 1967):359–367; *Frost: Centennial Essays* (1974); and Reginald Cook, *Robert Frost: A Living Voice* (1974), especially pp. 263–267. Brower is excellent on the shifting tones of voice, for example, from what he calls "the cheerfully observant walker on back country roads" who reports "I found a dimpled . . ."—but then comes the surprising "spider, fat and white"—to the "self-questioning and increasingly serious" sestet. Here, for Brower, "the first question ('What had the flower to do . . . ') sounds like ordinary annoyance at a fact that doesn't fit in." The next question brings in a new note, and irony in "kindred." For Brower, with the last question ironic puzzlement turns into vision: "What but design of darkness to appall?" And then Brower says that in the final line "The natural theologian pauses—he is only asking, not asserting—and takes a backward step."

The title echoes the "Argument from Design," the argument that the universe is designed (each creature fits perfectly into its environment: the whale is equipped for the sea; the camel for the desert), so there must be a designer, God. Notice that the word *design* has two meanings: (1) pattern and (2) intention, plan. Frost certainly means us to have both meanings in mind: there seems to be a pattern and also an intention behind it, but this intention is quite different from the intention discerned by those who in the eighteenth and nineteenth centuries argued for the existence of a benevolent God from the "Argument from Design."

"Design" was published in 1922; below is an early 1912 version of the poem, entitled "In White":

A dented spider like a snow drop white
On a white Heal-all, holding up a moth

Like a white piece of lifeless satin cloth—
Saw ever curious eye so strange a sight?—
Portent in little, assorted death and blight
Like the ingredients of a witches' broth?—
The beady spider, the flower like a froth,
And the moth carried like a paper kite.

What had that flower to do with being white?
The blue prunella every child's delight.
What brought the kindred spider to that height?
(Make we no thesis of the miller's plight.)
What but design of darkness and of night?
Design, design! Do I use the word aright?

The changes, obvious enough, are discussed by George Monteiro, in *Frost: Centennial Essays* (1974), published by the Committee on the Frost Centennial of the University of Southern Mississippi, pp. 35–38.

By the way, an ingenious student mentioned that the first stanza has eight lines, corresponding to the eight legs of a spider. And the second stanza has six, corresponding to the six legs of a moth. What to do? We tried to talk about the traditional structure of the sonnet, and about relevant and irrelevant conjectures, and about the broad overlapping area. About as good a criterion as any is, does the conjecture make the poem better?